BURN

THE LIFE STORY OF FIRE

TANYA LLOYD KYI

annick press
toronto + new york + var

Annick Press Ltd.

We acknowledge the support of the Canada Council for the Arts, the Ontario Arts Council, and the Government of Canada through the Book Publishing Industry Development Program (BPIDP) for our publishing activities.

Edited by Pam Robertson
Copy edited by Elizabeth McLean
Cover design by Kong Njo
Interior design by Vancouver Desktop Publishing Centre
Cover photogragh: © istockphoto.com/Timothy Goodwin
Interior illustrations:
(chapter opening photo) © istockphoto.com/Sascha Burkard;
(flame background) © istockphoto.com/Boris Zaytsev;
(fire sprite) © istockphoto.com/Thomas Paschke

Cataloguing in Publication

Kyi, Tanya Lloyd, 1973–
    Burn : the life story of fire / by Tanya Lloyd Kyi.

Includes bibliographical references and index.
ISBN 978-1-55451-082-5 (bound)
ISBN 978-1-55451-081-8 (pbk.)

    1. Fire—History—Juvenile literature.
2. Civilization—History—Juvenile
literature. I. Title.

TP265.K95 2007   304.2   C2007-901150-0

Printed and bound in Canada

Annick Press is committed to protecting our natural environment. As part of our efforts, this book is printed on Enviro paper: it contains 30% post-consumer recycled fibers, is acid-free, and is processed chlorine-free.

Published in the U.S.A. by Annick Press (U.S.) Ltd.

Distributed in Canada by	Distributed in the U.S.A. by
Firefly Books Ltd.	Firefly Books (U.S.) Inc.
66 Leek Crescent	P.O. Box 1338
Richmond Hill, ON	Ellicott Station
L4B 1H1	Buffalo, NY 14205

Visit our website at **www.annickpress.com**

CONTENTS

The First Sparks

Thirteen-year-old Michele McBride was struggling with a math assignment on December 1, 1958, when someone shouted from the back of the room. Swiveling in their chairs, the students saw a boy named Jeff with his hands pressed against the rear door.

The nun in charge swept toward the door at the front and yanked it open. Immediately, a cloud of black smoke poured into the room. Fire! The nun quickly slammed the door shut and students rushed to help fill the gap at the bottom with sweaters and scarves.

But it was already too late. The air inside the room was thick and hot. Michele struggled to say her rosary, as the nun suggested, and wondered how long it would take for firefighters to arrive. Around her, the classroom disintegrated into chaos. Students knocked over their desks in a rush toward the windows, but only the small ones in the top row of windows actually opened. Some students panicked and screamed. Others climbed on the sills and pressed their faces to the small gaps, yelling across the courtyard to the other classrooms.

"Fire! The school's on fire!"

As the air grew harder to breathe, one of the boys grabbed the long metal pole that was used to open and close the highest windows. Brandishing it like a spear, he bashed it against one of the lower ones until the glass shattered. Michele looked on with relief, thinking fresh air would rush in—but instead, black smoke poured out. The students pressed closer and closer to the windowsills.

Pushing people out of the way, a boy named Teddy yelled, "I'm getting out of here." He stepped through the jagged glass and leaped into the air, landing on an awning a story below. Then, grabbing a drainpipe, he swung down until he could jump the final distance to the ground. As he ran off to find help, several other students copied his maneuver.

Michele was too scared to jump—it was too far to the ground and the students nearest the windows were pushing and shoving one another. But behind her in the classroom, children were slapping their skin as the sweltering heat began to sting.

When she looked out the window again, men had tied two ladders together to try to reach the second story. But as soon as the first girl stepped onto the rungs, the joint between the ladders buckled, and she went crashing to the ground. Finally, firefighters arrived. But their ladders weren't high enough either!

Coughing and crying, alternating between standing crushed at the window for air and resting in the smoke of the classroom, Michele could see no way out. Then, suddenly, a blaze of orange filled the room and the clothes on her back seemed as if they were alive. The flames had burst in and attacked the desks, the floor, the students' clothing. Without thinking, Michele scrambled to the window a final time and hurled herself outside.

The fire at Our Lady of the Angels School began about two p.m., in a wastepaper basket at the bottom of the basement stairs. Several boys smelled smoke in the hallways and a few nearby classrooms were evacuated, but because the principal was away and no one could find the source of the smell, the fire alarm wasn't pulled. By the time students in other classrooms smelled or felt the blaze, the hallways and stairwells were filled with smoke. The orderly escape marches they had practiced in their fire drills were useless.

A nearby store owner called the fire department, but when firefighters arrived they were trapped outside the courtyard by an iron fence. By the time they tore down the barricade, they found there were too few men to hoist the heavy aluminum ladders or hold nets to catch the jumping students. The few adults who gathered on the ground held out their arms to try to catch the children, or lay down on the ground to try to cushion their falls.

When the fire hoses finally doused the flames, 92 children and three nuns were dead. Another 75 students lay injured at seven different hospitals in the Chicago area. After searching through the crowds of children outside the school, then driving from hospital to hospital, Michele's mother and father eventually found her at Saint Anne's Hospital, wrapped in bandages. She had a fractured skull and third-degree burns. But after four months of skin grafts and antibiotics, she was allowed to go home for the first time at Easter. As an adult, she founded a rehabilitation program for burn victims.

The effects of this school fire reached far outside Chicago. People from around the world—including Pope John XXIII—sent messages of sympathy. In the Soviet Union, the government criticized the United States for spending more money on weapons than it did on school safety. And within the country, officials took a close look at other elementary schools. By the following spring, 16,500 schools had been renovated to improve fire safety.

To survivors of the fire, the messages and statistics were of little interest. They would spend the rest of their lives remembering the thick smell of smoke, the feeling of heat searing their lungs, and the sounds of their classmates screaming. Fire was no longer an abstract presence in their lives—it was a threatening, lurking danger.

THE SCIENCE OF SPARKS

No one was ever charged with starting the fire at Our Lady of Angels elementary school, but investigators believed it was deliberately set. They determined that a student had struck a match and held it to the edge of a piece of crumpled paper until it caught. Then he or she dropped the burning paper into a wastepaper basket in the stairwell, setting the basket, and eventually the entire school, on fire.

After such a tragedy, it's the job of fire investigators to comb through the remains and decide what went wrong, and what could be done differently in the future. In a police investigation, detectives can cordon off entire scenes and sift through every object in an apartment or a building. But for fire investigators, there are often only ashes and smoke stains to use as guides.

They begin by interviewing witnesses. Where did the fire appear to start? Who raised the alarm? What time did you first smell the smoke? They also speak with firefighters. What time did you receive the call? Who were the last people in the building?

Once they've gathered as many accounts as possible,

investigators follow clues to the source of the flames. In the most destroyed area of the building, they look for signs. Was this where the fire began? Or is the room more damaged because oil or other flammable material was stored here? They might analyze the path of the fire by examining what is left of walls and furniture. One side of this dresser is burned, the other side intact. Why? Why are the beams black on the south side, but not on the north?

By tracing these clues, they can often find the place where the fire began. Then they begin, like archeologists, sifting through the dust. If they find a piece of wire, it's possible a bomb was used to spark the blaze. If they find a blackened motor, maybe a piece of equipment caused a spark. In some cases, investigators even recreate a scene—a cluttered office or a row of theater seats—and measure how long a fire would take to become unstoppable.

Firefighters use a pyramid to help explain the science of fire. The three sides of the pyramid are the ingredients necessary to maintain a flame—heat, fuel, and oxygen. At the base of the pyramid is the chemical reaction: the process that turns energy locked inside a strip of paper, a piece of wood, or a barrel of oil into the light and heat of a fire. For firefighters, the pyramid model makes it easier to understand how best to stop a blaze. If they can remove any side of the pyramid—use water to control the heat, or clear a firebreak to remove the fuel—the fire will collapse.

But just because we understand how fire functions doesn't always mean we can prevent it. Today we have sprinkler systems in ceilings, smoke alarms connected directly to fire halls, fire extinguishers in almost every building, and yet sparks still ignite, smolder, and burn so quickly out of control that no one can stop them. Each year, there are 7 million building fires around the world. About 4000 people are killed in the United States, more than 350 in Canada, and more than 100 in Australia. We also have satellites to monitor our forests, yet millions of dollars in property are lost and hundreds of forests are destroyed annually.

Like earthquakes or hurricanes, fires are one of the natural dangers in the world that humans haven't learned to control. And because flames are so difficult to predict, and yet so present in our daily lives, stories of fire continue to fascinate us. When we hear about a fire like the one at Our Lady of the

Birthday Candles and Evil Spirits

In Germany in the 1400s, families believed that children on their birthdays were in danger from evil spirits. To protect the little ones, candles were lit on a cake and kept burning all day and all through dinner, frightening the spirits away and carrying prayers and wishes to God. Finally, as evening fell and the danger passed, the candles were extinguished and the cake served— the beginning of a birthday tradition that has lasted until modern times.

Angels School, we don't stop to think about the process of the chemical reaction. We think of how the students must have felt, trapped between the fire and the fall. We feel the smoke filling our throats and pressing against our chests.

Thousands of years ago, people considered fire a powerful mystery a force to be worshiped and feared. Today, our views haven't changed that much.

ALL FIRED UP

When we think of fire, it's natural to focus on its destructive side—forest fires sweeping through mountain valleys or house fires devastating families. But we rarely stop to think about fire's more positive roles. Since prehistoric times, it has drawn people close on dark nights. For those such as the Inuit of northern Canada, a central fire in each tent or igloo made it possible to exist through cold, sunless winters, to work and sew, and to gather for stories or dancing. And even today, campers gather around fires to eat and share tales. The warmth and cheer of a flame naturally brings people together.

As tiny children, less aware of the dangers of flame, we're fascinated by candles on our birthday cake, the embers of a campfire, or the sudden flare of a match. As we grow older, we lose some of that sense of awe. And we forget that fire is essential to our civilization, both as a symbol and as a tool.

When we hear the rumble of the furnace starting in the morning, or turn on the burner of the gas stove, or light the candles on the dinner table, we're using fire the same ways early humans did hundreds of thousands of years ago—for heat, food, and light. And when we eat off ceramic dinner plates, walk across a concrete floor, or gaze out a glass window, we're using materials formed with flame.

Although it has the power to destroy almost anything in its path, fire also has the power to renew forests or, in the case of molten rock, to create new land. It has served as one of the most essential tools in the development of human civilization, giving birth to countless inventions and industries, and it's one of religion's most enduring symbols. On a more personal scale, it affects how we eat, how we dress, and how we see. From the lighting of a baptism candle to the kindling of a funeral pyre, it's present in every moment of human life.

In fact, fire has been so important to people throughout history that many cultures believed it was one of the basic foundations of the world. According to traditional Chinese beliefs, the natural world was composed of five elements: earth, metal, water, wood, and fire. If one element outweighed another, the world was thrown out of balance. A fever, for example, might have been a sign that fire had taken greater control in the body. Hinduism also includes the belief that fire is an element of all living things, along with water, wind, sky, and earth.

In Europe, similar beliefs stemmed from the studies of a philosopher in Sicily named Empedocles. Seven thousand years ago, he was renowned for his miracles and claimed to be able to control the wind and bring the dead back to life. (According to some tales, he died when he jumped into a volcano, trying to prove he was a god.) Empedocles believed that all matter was made up of four elements: earth, air, water, and fire. His idea was adopted by the ancient Greek philosopher Aristotle, and was commonly accepted until the 1700s. It wasn't until a French scientist named Antoine Laurent Lavoisier began studying combustion in the 1770s that the world learned that fires involved fuels reacting with oxygen.

After Lavoisier's studies, scientists no longer called fire one of the four vital elements of life. Yet the Earth itself has a fiery core and the power of flame stretches from volcano craters to car engines. Our homes are heated with fire, our industries run on flames, and our hearts fall in love over candlelight. It may not be a basic element of the human body, but it's certainly a vital part of human life.

ONE

Fanning the Flames

FIRE AND CIVILIZATION

Gray Eagle once ruled the world, controlling sun, moon, water, and fire. He kept these treasures to himself and hung them on the sides of his lodge where only he and his family could enjoy them. Gray Eagle spared no attention for humans, those weak creatures who roamed the Pacific coast in darkness.

But Gray Eagle had a daughter, and her beauty caught the eye of a handsome being named Raven. Changing himself into a white bird, Raven pursued the eagle's daughter until she fell in love and invited him back to the lodge to meet her father.

Raven flew to the meeting filled with excitement, thinking only of romance. But then he saw the lodge. He saw sun, moon, water, and fire hung on the walls, and he thought of the people struggling to survive in darkness. Immediately, Raven knew that he would have to sacrifice his love for the sake of humans.

Sweeping toward the wall, he plucked up the treasures in his beak. Then, soaring high into the air, he hung the sun where it would illuminate the world. Guided by this new light, Raven flew far across the ocean. There, he hung the moon. Then Raven glided back to the land and sprinkled the water across it, creating streams, rivers, and lakes.

By this time, the fire in Raven's beak was burning and smoking. It charred his face and sent smoke pouring over his feathers. Raven tried to bear the pain while he found the perfect home for fire, but eventually, the flames grew too hot. He dropped fire onto mountain rocks, where it disappeared from sight.

Raven's feathers never recovered. They are black to this day. And even now, when people strike two rocks together in just the right way, they see the spark of the fire treasure Raven stole from Gray Eagle.

SPARKING IDEAS

Fire may not have arrived on the Earth in the beak of a raven as stories from North America's Pacific coast tell us, but it has been a key force in the development of human civilization. It allows us to cook our food, heat and illuminate our homes, and gather to share ideas with our friends and families. And it began serving these purposes a million years ago.

In 1947, Scottish-born doctor and paleontologist Robert Bloom was exploring a site near Johannesburg, South Africa, when he came upon a human skull different from anything he had seen before. As he dug further, he found more bones—human and animal—as well as tools. Bloom had discovered the opening to a limestone cave now known as Swartkrans (and part of the Cradle of Humankind World Heritage Site).

Scientists began to carefully excavate the cave, brushing away centuries of dirt to find each bone and artifact. As they dug deeper, they found remains from 500,000 years ago, then from twice that far into the past. And mixed with all of the human bones and tools was evidence of charcoal. Even a million years ago, the humans who lived in the area were using fire to cook their food.

But the scientists kept digging. They dug and dug until the remains they were finding were 3.3 million years old. They noticed that once they passed the 1 million year level, there were no more signs of charcoal. And below that level, there were more gnawed bones of humans and less gnawed animal remains. It appeared that before humans began using fire, *they* were more often the prey. Then, once they controlled the flames, they became the hunters.

A million years ago, early humans like the ones who lived near Swartkrans probably gathered and ate the charred bodies of animals killed by wildfires. Archeological finds also suggest that when people found burning wood from a wildfire or lightning strike, they used the flames to cook or to harden weapons. Still later, people managed to gather coals from passing wildfires and slowly feed them, nestling them inside a horn, shell, or coconut husk. These embers were so precious they would be tended constantly and carried from one camp to the next.

This ability to keep a fire burning opened new worlds of abilities—people could warm themselves, see after nightfall, scare away wild animals, hunt large animals by herding them with brush fires, clear land for agriculture, harden spears, and signal to each other from hilltop to hilltop.

Of course, keeping a coal continually lit while traveling across the plains or the mountains wasn't always easy. Archeologists still don't know exactly where or when it happened, but people eventually learned to create their own flames. Around the world, different tribes discovered that the easiest way to actually create fire is to produce enough friction to make a spark, then fan that spark onto a pile of dry tinder, such as old moss or wood shavings.

Today, a young Boy Scout might have to work until his arms ache before he produces a spark by rubbing two sticks together. People in primitive tribes could do it in mere minutes. In Australia, they would saw one piece of wood back and forth across another. On the islands of the South Pacific, they would push a stick back and forth like a plow into a grooved piece of wood. And in Africa, they would twirl a stick between their palms, resting the end on a flat piece of wood.

Like the Native people who believed that Raven had dropped his fire on the rocks, some societies about 2000 years ago discovered that by striking flint (a type of stone) on steel, they could create a spark. This was much faster than creating friction with sticks, and the method eventually spread around the world. For centuries, a set rested beside every hearth, and European gentlemen carried small lighting kits in their pockets.

Although flint and steel seems hopelessly obsolete today, it was the first fast, reliable, and portable way humans knew

Sparks for Sale

In Canada, traders with the Hudson's Bay Company routinely carried supplies of flint and steel strike-a-lights, to offer in trade for furs with Native hunters.

to create fire. The flare of a match and the flick of a barbecue lighter were still generations away.

In 1680, an Irish scientist named Robert Boyle was experimenting with a recently discovered mineral— phosphorous—when he discovered that if he rubbed a piece of sulfur-coated wood against it, it would create a small flame. "How interesting," he thought . . . and that was the end of experimentation until 1827. That's when an English pharmacist named John Walker coated some wooden sticks with the chemicals antimony sulfide, potassium chlorate, gum, and starch. When they dried, he could rub them against any rough surface and they would burst into flame. John sold his invention under the catchy name of Sulpheretted Peroxide Strikeables. There was just one disadvantage—each stick was as long as a man's arm.

Still, Walker's matches sparked a few ideas when people saw them. Soon, a man named Samuel Jones was selling smaller versions, ideal for smokers. Too bad they smelled like rotten eggs. Next, French chemist Charles Sauria got rid of the stink by inventing a match that used white phosphorous. What he didn't know was that white phosphorous was extremely poisonous. Soon, workers in match factories were suffering from a type of cancer called phossy jaw—their

Hazardous to Your Health

When smokers bought their supplies in the 1800s, it was the matches, not the cigarettes, that carried a health warning.

gums swelled, their teeth fell out, then their jawbones became infected and began rotting away. Children who chewed on matchsticks suffered bone damage, girls selling matchbooks lost their hair, and heavy smokers experienced brain damage.

Once people finally figured out the phosphorous and phossy jaw connection, Swedish inventor Johan Edvard Lundstrom came up with matches that didn't use white phosphorous. Instead, each box had a strip of red phosphorous on the outside for lighting the matchstick. The first matchbook followed in 1889, and in 1910, the Diamond Match Company of the United States patented the first non-stinky, non-poisonous matches. American president William H. Taft was so impressed that he asked the company to give up the patent and release the match formula for the good of people around the world.

Today, humans use 500 billion matches a year. But the quest to control fire—to have flames appear at our fingertips—has led us away from matches and toward lighters. With a flick of friction we light a small stream of gas. Our stoves and our barbecues burn for us with just the press of a button, and our fireplaces no longer need flint and steel kits—we can ignite the gas by flicking the switch on the wall. But all these instant fires serve the same purposes that prehistoric fires did. They allow us to cook, to have heat and light in our homes, and to curl up and chat by the hearth. Only our methods have changed.

THE GREAT HUNT

While no one knows exactly when humans learned to create fire, in Europe, North and South America, Asia, and Australia, archeologists have found evidence of torches, firepits, and fiery hunting grounds that date back hundreds of thousands of years.

The region of Torralba, Spain, was a huge tropical swamp 250,000 years ago. Finding that elephants wandering into the sticky mud were trapped, prehistoric humans quickly developed a way to herd the animals toward danger. They would light the brush behind a herd, and wait for the elephants to stampede and mire themselves in the swamp where they could be speared easily. Then, using wooden and stone axes and scrapers, they would carve the meat off the animals. Charcoal found at the site suggests that people used fire to cook the meat as well as to herd the beasts.

In far distant corners of the world, people hunted in very similar ways. In 1700, a British man named John Lawson traveled to what is now North Carolina and hiked his way across the state, mapping the forests and writing about the customs of the Native people he met. Several times, he described how people used fire to hunt, setting the marshes ablaze to drive out hares, or chasing animals into hollow logs, then smoking them out. As temperatures cooled in the fall, Lawson was surprised to notice tribes journeying for several days to gather near the coast. Slowly, they congregated in a massive camp, until there were 200, then 300 people present. Lawson learned that they were preparing for a hunt.

When the day came, hunters spread themselves around the edges of a peninsula. Some waited on the beaches with bows, while others skirted the land in their canoes, armed with spears. Then, at the line where the peninsula met the mainland, people set the leaves on the forest floor alight. Dry from the long, hot summer, the leaves cracked and burned, the flames roaring quickly along the ground but not reaching high enough to burn many of the taller trees. Smoke billowed into the sky.

From out of the forest, fleeing the flames and hoping for the safety of the water, came elk, deer, moose, and countless small animals—only to find themselves penned by the hunters along the shore. Within a few hours, the men had slaughtered enough animals to provide all the people who had traveled to the hunt with enough meat to last through the winter. Tribes returned to their own settlements laden with food.

The hunting practices that Lawson observed in North Carolina were common throughout the continent. On the plains, people used fire to herd buffalo toward cliffs, and on the tundra, they drove muskrats from their dens. People hunted with fire in other parts of the world, as well. In Venezuela, hunters set hillsides on fire to clear the brush and expose the hiding places of yellow-footed tortoises, nicely baked in their shells by the flames. And Aboriginal people in Australia hunted kangaroos by trapping them in circles of flaming brush. To all of these people, the hunt was a focal point of life, and tools that made it successful—tools such as fire—were treasured.

Sparks with Side Effects

Hunting with fire did more than drive game toward swamps or cliffs. It also cleared the land. The next year, even more game would return to the area to eat the tender new growth at the burn site.

Just as early hunters adapted fire to their needs, so did the first herders and farmers. In Scandinavia, tribes loosely herded reindeer, following the food supply and migrating with the beasts. When biting flies and fleas drove the herds into constant motion, these shepherds sometimes used large smudge fires to drive away the bugs and allow the reindeer to rest.

In Australia, the strongest and smartest men were given the task of setting brush fires, often burning different parts of the forest every three to five years. They would spark their flames carefully, then patrol the edges with long green boughs, ready to beat out any flames that escaped in the wrong direction. By using fire this way, they were able to ensure a steady supply of tender new plants—the easiest to gather and eat. They also kept travel routes free of undergrowth and debris. Meanwhile, early farmers around the world discovered that flames could both clear land and provide nutrients for the soil.

NOW WE'RE COOKIN'

By burning brush, shepherding animals, or clearing land, early humans were able to use fire to harvest more food. But they also used it to prepare that food, in ways that may have changed all of human evolution.

A Harvard University anthropologist named Richard Wrangham spent years studying the diets of early humans and modern monkeys. He even followed a family of chimpanzees through the jungles of Africa, gnawing on the same plants they did. He discovered that it took strong teeth, large jaws, and a lot of time to eat enough raw food to sustain human life.

Wrangham pointed out that about 20 million years ago, early humans' brains were growing (to double the size of ape brains), their jaws were shrinking, and they were growing larger and taller. He and his colleagues believed these changes happened because humans began cooking their foods. As soon as these early chefs began using flames to char meat and soften tubers, meat became safer, proteins were more easily digested, and plants that had been poisonous when raw could now be cooked and eaten.

Some scientists disagreed with Wrangham, and many disagreed with his timelines. After all, the earliest pit ovens date from only 1.5 million years ago in Africa and 300,000 years ago in Europe. But Wrangham insisted that changes in people's teeth and body size prove they were cooking long before that. He continues to research, and promised that as more discoveries are made, more answers will surface.

Whether or not it changed all of human evolution, we do know that cooking was discovered and used in different ways

Hot Stuff

Our modern cooking methods range from the most primitive—open barbecue flames in the backyard—to the most sophisticated uses of microwaves and radiation. Induction ranges even create heat using electricity and magnetism instead of fire.

around the globe. In Hawaii, people dug large pits and built bonfires inside, covering the fires with a layer of volcanic rock. As the wood burned, the rocks would turn white from the heat and settle to rest at the base of the pit. After stuffing a whole pig with extra heated rocks, they would lower the meat into the pit, cover it with banana leaves, and shovel a mound of dirt on top, trapping the heat and steam inside the pit. Half a day later, the meat would be roasted and tender.

In Australia, early European explorers watched as Aboriginals used similar ovens to cook a type of flatbread, first grinding seeds into flour, then mixing the flour with water and laying the dough on leaves over the coals.

Other cultures developed cooking methods according to their needs and resources. Historians believe the first teas were brewed in Tibet and western China about 2700 BCE. About 2000 BCE, in the deserts of the Middle East, people learned to use fire to boil and purify water. And in 1500 BCE, Egyptians fermented yeast to make bread. Two hundred years later, someone in China started a tradition that would last until today—he scribbled down the ingredients for marinated spiced carp, creating the first written recipe.

HOME IS WHERE THE HEAT IS

The ability to use fire caused huge changes in the lives of early humans. Instead of eating wherever their hunted animals happened to fall, or wherever the berry bushes were found, they gathered food and carried it to a central fire. Archeologists speculate that when humans first began to capture and use coals, fire was so valuable that only one central fire would be tended for each tribe, and everyone would gather and cook around the same blaze. But gradually, as they gained greater control and even the ability to spark their own flames, people began to incorporate fire into individual homes. Just as a teepee has a central opening at the top to allow smoke to escape, many early dwellings were created around a central firepit, or hearth.

Incorporating heat into their homes allowed people to live in new areas. Mountain slopes and northern forests that had once been too cold for survival became new hunting grounds. People migrated from the warmth of the Mediterranean to the chilly climates of Britain before the island broke from the mainland—before the English Channel existed. By about 11,000 years ago, humans were even living in northern Siberia, within the Arctic Circle.

It didn't take long for people to discover that fire was as useful for light as it was for heat. Archeologists have found the remains of torches in caves from tens of thousands of years ago, as well as hollowed stones that may have served as primitive candles. Such stones have been found in caves in Spain where some of the most elaborate examples of cave art have been discovered—art painted by the flickering light of animal fat candles.

Early humans burned small containers of animal fat, and

Fish Sticks on Fire

Along the Pacific coast of North America, Native people burned a type of fish called the oolichan, or candlefish. The fish was so rich in oil that it could be dried, then skewered on a stick and lit.

ancient Egyptians burned rushes dipped into fat. People in Tibet used yak butter as candle fuel. But it was the Romans who finally invented the candle as we know it today, with a wick in the center. They didn't replace the animal fat, though—not until the Middle Ages, when beeswax was adopted. In the years since, candles have been made with berry extracts, whale blubber, and paraffin, a wax made from petroleum.

In the 1830s, industrialists began manufacturing molded wax candles in factories, but their success was short-lived. Twenty years later, petroleum oil was distilled into kerosene, which proved to be a cheap, clean-burning fuel for lamps and lanterns. Soon, candles were used mostly for decoration and kerosene lamps lit every kitchen. They lasted until 1879, when Thomas Edison produced the first reliable electric light bulbs.

Now, as we turn on our houselights with a flick of a switch, we can forget that fire is lighting our homes. But not only are tiny filaments burning inside the light bulbs—massive power plants are churning through coal just to keep them lit. One coal-fired plant in southern Indiana produces more power than the Hoover Dam—enough to supply 3 million people. It burns 300 train cars of coal per day. In China, power plants struggling to provide enough energy for a booming population consume over a billion tonnes each year. Just because we don't necessarily see the fire heating and lighting our homes doesn't mean it's not burning . . . somewhere.

CREATURE COMFORTS

As people adapted to fire and began to mold their lives around its use, its warmth and light began to represent comfort. Today, we still consider the crackling of an open fire a symbol of relaxation. And for thousands of years, when people have spoken of "hearth and home," they have thought of the shelter of their own homes, warmed by their own fires.

As a symbol of power and a symbol of community, fire played an important role in many early cultures. The Iroquois people of eastern North America held their councils around a blazing flame, sometimes praying and dancing around the same fire if major decisions were reached or wars were declared. In the 16th century, as American settlers encroached on the land and Native groups struggled to find their places in a changing continent, a leader named Hiawatha convinced five tribes to bind themselves together as one Iroquois Confederacy. Forming the geographic and political center of the group was the Onondagas tribe. To

Safety Savvy

For early humans, fires kept wild animals at bay. Now we depend on lights to keep criminals at bay. The first streetlights were hung by the mayor of London in 1417 and were made by enclosing candles in glass domes. Inventor Benjamin Franklin later improved the lamps by designing a new shape with vents that allowed smoke to escape and the candles to burn more brightly.

emphasize their role as a respected group and as the hosts of communal gatherings, Hiawatha named them the keepers of the council fire.

All over the world, throughout history, fire created stronger human communities, first by bringing people together to eat, then by providing the warmth and light by which we could dance, tell stories, and share ideas. According to the ancient Greeks, fire was the gift that made humans more like the gods, and better able to succeed in a cold, harsh world.

Legend tells us that Zeus, creator of thunder and lightning and ruler of the gods, asked Prometheus and Epimetheus to fill the Earth with living creatures. Epimetheus eagerly set about his task, populating the land, the oceans, and the air with all the animals he could imagine. Zeus had offered many gifts to make the task easier, and Epimetheus gave those gifts to his creations—wings to the birds, fur to the cats, and fins to the dolphins.

But while his brother was busily dividing up the gifts, Prometheus was still trying to perfect a masterpiece. He had spent the entire time on only one new species—humans. When they were finally complete, Prometheus was thrilled with his work. But none of Zeus's gifts remained to help the new creatures, and they were cold during the long, dark nights.

When Zeus refused to help the humans (after all, he had already offered plenty of talents), Prometheus decided to take matters into his own hands. He climbed Mount Olympus to the home of the gods and found the chariot that carried the sun across the sky. Stealing a flame from the chariot and hiding it in a hollow plant stalk, Prometheus carried it back down the mountain and presented it to humans. He taught them to use his gift for food, warmth, and light. And though Zeus punished Prometheus harshly for his disobedience, humans were able to thrive.

TWO

Burnings and Blessings

FIRE AND BELIEF

Thousands of years ago, the Hindu gods and spirits gathered for a great sacrifice and offered up the body of one of their own: Purusha. As he died, Purusha fell and his enormous body created the world. One of his eyes became the sun, his brain became the moon, his navel became the air, and his feet became the Earth. As the last breaths left him, two gods were spawned from his mouth: Indra, god of storms and thunder, and Agni, god of fire.

Born out of this grand sacrifice, Agni grew large and powerful, flowing through every aspect of the new planet. He became a sort of electricity, brought to Earth as lightning. He became the spark of life in human beings and the sap that moves and flows within plant life. He hid himself within sticks, but could be brought forth with friction. For the humans who walked the newly created land, Agni was a protector, providing warmth and light. Yet he was also dangerous enough to conquer entire villages or forests. Some people envisioned him as a lion who raced through the woods with his orange mane flying behind him, leaving only charred trees, smoke, and ashes in his wake.

Because Agni was so closely tied to people, he became a mediator between the realm of humans and the realm of the supernatural. When humans sacrificed animals or plants, he consumed the offerings and carried them to the heavens. And whenever they lit a flame—whether in the privacy of their homes or during the public celebration of a new marriage—Agni was there to bear witness, to watch over and nurture life.

LIFE-GIVING FIRE

For people who dedicated day and night to tending flames—finding fuel, nurturing embers, banking coals for the long evenings—fire became something to cherish. As well as worshiping flame itself, many cultures endowed their gods with the characteristics of fire. These supernatural beings have the ability to nurture life or to destroy, just as real fire does. Like hearth fires, they could be helpful when they were well looked after and awe-inspiring and dangerous when they grew out of human control. From their erratic moods and frightening wrath to their care for crops and sympathy for young lovers, the temperaments of these gods give us clues to how people viewed fire itself.

For the early people of eastern Europe, flame was a warrior called Svarozhich, a fierce fighter with glowing armor and a massive axe. He was the warmth of summer and the one responsible for the fire that dried the ripened corn and wheat each fall. Because he existed within the flames, a person who spit into a fire could face endless bad fortune.

In ancient Persia, the god of flame was named Atar and

he lived both in the sky and within wood. Like Svarozhich, he was a fierce destroyer yet a generous provider, bringing people comfort, survival skills, and wisdom. He accompanied the sun's chariot across the sky, protected the world from evil, and guided the dead to the afterworld.

To people of Japan, Ho-Masubi appeared either as a yellow and orange man with fiery hair or a swift, impulsive wild boar. He was generally a friendly spirit, providing humans with warmth and light, the power to mold metal and forge tools, and the ability to cook their food. But if he was neglected, Ho-Masubi could quickly turn destructive. His wrath could char a home or an entire settlement with lightning speed.

Eastern Europeans no longer dry their crops over open fires and the people of Iran no longer believe the sun rides in a chariot. But not all fire gods are from the ancient past; some are actively worshiped today. The god Agni of the Hindu faith, a being written about in hymns hundreds of years old, remains a powerful force in many people's lives today. They believe that because fires are relit every day, Agni remains

Fact or Fiction?

Some scientists think the biblical burning bush could have been *Dictamnus fraxinella*, a shrub that gives off a flammable vapor on sunny days. The vapor itself could have burned without consuming the bush.

young for eternity. But because fire will always exist on the Earth, he is also immortal.

Even cultures that don't worship flames directly often believe that gods and angels can appear in fire. In the Christian Bible, a man named Moses was tending a herd of sheep in the Egyptian desert when a nearby bush burst into flame. To his astonishment, the bush wasn't harmed by the fire. Instead, an angel appeared within the blaze, telling Moses to lead his people out of Egypt toward a promised land that God had prepared for them.

A LIGHT IN THE DARKNESS

Fire has also been used as a symbol in religious traditions and rituals. Jewish people believe that in ancient times a seven-candle menorah (a holy, branched candleholder), remained lit for eight days when there was only enough fuel to burn for one. In celebration of this miracle, they light the nine-candle Chanukkiyah—a variation of the menorah—during the annual holiday of Hanukkah.

In the Christian faith, the candles of the advent wreath are lit during the weeks before Christmas to symbolize hope, faith, and joy. And for Orthodox Christians, a holy flame lit once a year serves as a reminder that miracles can happen.

On the day before Easter in the Orthodox Christian calendar, an archbishop in Jerusalem recites a prayer. He then enters the tomb of Jesus, where Christ is believed to have been buried, holding an unlit olive oil lamp. Outside, the faithful chant, "Lord, have mercy. Lord, have mercy." The scene is broadcast live on international television to millions of Christians.

Each year when the archbishop emerges from the tomb, his lamp is miraculously alight.

The annual lighting of this holy flame in Jerusalem has

been documented since 1106. Skeptics have gone to great lengths to disprove the miracle: Turkish soldiers and Israeli officials have searched the body of the archbishop, to ensure he wasn't carrying matches or flint; scientists have dipped torches in white phosphorus and demonstrated that it bursts into flames after 20 minutes or so in the open air; others have attributed the flame to static electricity or ball lightning. But to Orthodox Christians, each year's fire is a new miracle, and a sign that God is present in their lives.

After death, fire can represent a route of passage to the afterlife; the same way a sacrifice consumed by fire is thought to have been taken by the gods, a body in a funeral pyre is being sent to heaven. While Christian churches forbade cremation for centuries, calling it a pagan ritual, many Hindu and Buddhist societies have always burned their dead.

No Boys Allowed

In Kildare, Ireland, a sacred flame was tended by Celtic priestesses for hundreds of years. When Christianity reached the region in the fifth century, the shrine became a convent and nuns continued nurturing the fire for another 800 years. Only in 1220, when the archbishop of Dublin grew angry that no men were allowed into the convent, was the flame extinguished.

In India's holy city of Varanasi, permanent platforms at the edge of the sacred Ganges River allow mourners to gather near the funeral pyres as the bodies of their loved ones are offered to the gods.

There are many theories about why fire is used as a symbol in so many religious ceremonies, from baptisms and bar mitzvahs to communions and funerals. Some people believe that it offers comfort, the same way a hearth fire does. Others believe that when people's lives are difficult or confusing, the light of a candle guides them toward God, like a light in a house window might guide lost travelers to safety. Still others believe we appreciate candle flames because they are temporary; as the wicks burn away, they carry prayers toward heaven. For many worshipers, a flame might represent all of these things, and more.

THE FIRES OF HELL

The warm flicker of candles may serve as religious emblems, but the seething fires of hell are an entirely different kind of symbol. The Christian Bible calls hell "the fire that shall never be quenched," a place where Lucifer (whose name means "fire-bearer") and his followers are eternally tortured. They suffer in flames that burn without killing them. And people who don't believe in God will join the demons there. In the book of Luke, a rich man who has gone to hell cries out, "Father Abraham, have mercy on me, and send Lazarus, that he may dip the tip of his finger in water, and cool my tongue, for I am tormented in this flame."

The concept of a fiery underworld is far from unique. In Greek mythology, the River Phlegethon (a name that means "burning") is a tributary of the River Styx in the underworld Hades. In Jewish literature, a work called the *Book of the*

Secrets of Enoch tells of a tour of hell. Guided by two angels, Enoch sees a burning river, torture chambers lit by murky flames, and rooms filled with both fire and ice. And in Islamic tradition, faithful people spend eternity in a lush garden while sinners are tortured in the fires of a multilevel hell.

Just as it's not hard to imagine how a candle might remind people of comfort and safety, it's also not difficult to see how ancient writers might have adopted fire as a symbol of death and punishment. One of the Hebrew words that the writers of the New Testament used for "hell" was *gehenna*, the name for a city dump outside Jerusalem in the time of Jesus. To make sure the bodies of animals and criminals piled in the dump were completely burned, officials added sulfur to the mounds of refuse. The chemical made the dump burn continuously, even in the rain. To those living inside the city, it must have looked like the ultimate setting for eternal suffering. And to writers struggling to describe the tortures of eternal damnation, it served as a perfect—and horrific—symbol.

SACRIFICIAL FLAMES

In many ways, the theory of a fiery hell where souls are punished might be easier for us to grasp than real, breathing humans sacrificed by fire. Yet societies such as the Aztecs of ancient Mexico are famous for their boiled victims and roasted prisoners. Anthropologists believe the Aztecs killed up to 20,000 victims a year. Some they killed quickly, while others they set on fire, pulling them out of the flames just before death to remove their hearts and sacrifice them separately. But there was no other choice under the Aztec religion. If the rituals stopped, it was believed that the sun would literally fail to rise.

Spanish soldiers gained an up-close and much too personal

look at Aztec traditions in the 1500s. They had arrived in 1519 at the white walls of Tenochtitlán, the capital city of the Aztecs. It rose from the center of a lake, glistening in the sun, with stunning causeways linking the metropolis to the land. And in a glance, the Spanish saw enough riches to support themselves and their families for generations. They set out to do what they normally did—conquer.

They failed dismally. After meeting the Aztec warriors in battle, only a few beaten soldiers remained along the lakeshore, gazing toward Tenochtitlán's highest pyramid. Drums echoed across the water and trumpets blared as 62 Spanish fighters were dragged up the steps of the temple. After a ritual of prayer and dance, Aztec priests forced the men onto their backs. With quick slices through the ribcages, the priests revealed the hearts of the captives. They pulled them, still beating, out of the bodies, set them on fire, and offered them up to the gods.

The hearts of enemy warriors were always burned for the Aztec gods—only through these offerings could people be assured of continued blessings. Because deities such as Huit-zilopochtli, the sun god, lived in 52-year cycles, the Aztec people needed to accumulate half a century of sacrifices to ensure his rebirth. They believed that if the gods weren't nurtured by enough human blood, they wouldn't have the strength to begin the cycle again.

When the half-century mark arrived in ancient Tenochtitlán, every fire in the city was extinguished. As night fell, the people waited in darkness. Midnight. A final worthy sacrifice—probably a warrior proven brave in battle—was carried to the top of the temple, his heart sliced out and offered. Then the city waited again. Would the sacrifices of the past 52 years, topped by the midnight ritual, be enough to nourish the gods? Would the sun rise?

When it did, the entire city broke into celebration. Atop the temple, the priests kindled a fire on the body of the sacrificed warrior. From this fire, flames were lit and carried into the city streets. Each hearth was rekindled from the sacrificial flame. The end of the world had been postponed once again.

Almost every religion in every part of the world has included the idea of sacrifice. Whether in praise, in repentance, or in hope of blessings, people have sacrificed everything from fruit and bread to their own children. And in many cases, these sacrifices were made with fire, perhaps because of the power of fire to consume or because of the way smoke rises toward the heavens.

Among modern religions, Hinduism remains most closely tied to the idea of sacrifice. From small household rituals, during which a cook might sprinkle a few grains of rice into the stove, to large community events, sacrifice is viewed as a way to praise and appease the gods.

In the ceremony called the Yanja, priests gather before large crowds to place offerings into sacred flames. Coconuts, clarified butter called ghee, sandalwood chips, flowers, yogurt, fabric, and fruit are all dropped into the fire. Once consumed by the flames, the items can be carried by Agni—fire god and messenger—to the all-powerful gods called the devas.

What are the faithful hoping for as they sprinkle rice into a stove or watch an offering burned? In some places, people think their gods—like those of the Aztecs—gain strength from these rituals. Others believe that gods accept sacrifices in exchange for gifts such as good harvests, or that gods who are distracted by sacrifices are more likely to leave humans to live in relative peace. Whatever their reasons, believers in all religions finish their sacrifices with hope for blessings. They hope their offerings will bring new beginnings, the same way a burned field offers fertile soil for future crops.

TRIAL BY FIRE

Unfortunately, the idea of using flames in cleansing rituals has led some people to think of fire as an ideal sort of trial—the guilty will burn and be cleansed of their sins. If they're extremely lucky, the innocent may be saved by their faith. Otherwise, they will certainly go straight to heaven after their lives are sacrificed.

In 1478, King Ferdinand and Queen Isabella of Spain were struggling to defend their kingdom against Muslim powers. They lived at a time when there was enormous conflict between the Muslim, Jewish, and Christian peoples of southern Europe, and they used that conflict to ban non-Catholics from many professions. They also enlisted the support of the Roman Catholic church and formed a court called the Spanish Inquisition. Dedicated to finding, judging, and punishing people who didn't believe Catholic teachings, the court was intended to purge Spain of "unholy" influences.

The first Inquisitor General of the Spanish Inquisition was Thomas de Torquemada, a respected and well-educated monk who was appointed to the post in 1478. For 15 years, he scoured the country for "heretics": people who followed other religions, people who spoke out against the church, or even people who criticized the Inquisition itself.

De Torquemada believed that heretical beliefs were like viruses. If they weren't found and destroyed, they could spread to other people. And if heretics weren't "cured"—if they didn't repent after torture or in the midst of a bonfire—they were destined for hell. He went to great lengths to stop the spread of this virus. To the Inquisitor General, that meant everything from burning non-Catholic books to imprisoning heretics in places where they could have no contact with the outside world.

As for the heretics themselves, there were only two ways to cure them: torture them until they gave up their beliefs, or burn them alive. Presumably, being roasted on an open fire before a crowd of onlookers would give heretics such a vivid glimpse of hell that they were sure to repent for their beliefs. Those who repented weren't likely to be saved from the flames, but maybe their souls would be spared a more eternal searing. The burnings had the additional side benefit of scaring the onlookers into greater religious devotion.

During de Torquemada's reign, about 9000 people were burned alive. They were tied atop piles of wood in public squares, set alight, and left to struggle and scream in full view of the city residents, as thick gray smoke rose into the air and the stench of burning flesh filtered through the streets.

The execution of so many people has made the Spanish Inquisition synonymous with death and cruelty. People think of it as one of the most dangerous regimes in history. But the Inquisition wasn't the first group to burn people who didn't conform to society's standards, and it wasn't the last.

Dark Magic

Witch hunts still occur in parts of the world today. In a few rural regions of Africa and India, convicted witches can still be burned alive.

Across Europe, from the 1400s to the 1700s, many women (and some men) were accused of practicing witchcraft.

Often, witches accused in rural Europe were midwives or healers who used herbs as well as prayers in their treatments. When a patient grew worse or a baby died, it was easy to blame the tragedy on the healer. People were accused of worshiping the devil, placing curses on their neighbors, and meeting at night to cook potions out of human flesh.

And it wasn't just uneducated farmers or villagers who believed in the power of witches. Official courts heard charges and sentenced people. In Scotland in the late 1500s, the king himself participated in witch hunts.

Over the 300 years that witchcraft trials were common, about 40,000 people were executed. Most often, that meant death by fire. Because people believed that witches could use sorcery to protect themselves from harm, only the most painful kind of death would force them to repent. In places where judges were lenient, family members or friends of the witches would be allowed to bring extra wood to the pyre, to encourage the fire and speed the death. In other places, green wood or a carefully constructed flame could prolong the execution until the witch died of heat exhaustion or smoke inhalation. And like the burnings during the Inquisition, witch burnings were public events, drawing crowds from across the countryside.

PURIFYING FLAMES

The Spanish Inquisition and the persecution of witches are extreme examples of fire being used to purify. In many cases, flames have been incorporated in much more innocent folk beliefs. They may still be intended to cleanse people of their sins, but without the burning of flesh.

In 19th-century Ireland at the height of the summer, huge bonfires would be lit on hilltops, inviting villagers to venture outside for a night of singing, dancing, and celebration. The young men would dare one another to leap the flames, and the youth who leaped the highest fire would be considered the hero of the night—the one who had conquered the evil spirits of the year. Once the fires simmered lower, the young women would jump them as well, hoping to guarantee themselves good and speedy marriages. As the festivities wound to a close, the men would light torches from the festival fire and race home to their hearths. The first to enter their houses without putting out the flames were promised a year of good fortune.

A similar ritual still exists in Iran. There, on the last Wednesday of the year according to the solar calendar, people pour onto the streets or gather in their backyards. With bonfires lit, they sing *Sorkhiyeh to az man, zardieh man az to*—"Give me your healthy glow and take my yellow color away." They are hoping to be cleansed of the year's bad luck and granted good luck for the times ahead.

This view of fire as a way to purify people is common to many faiths. And along with such purity can come extraordinary power over flame. On Beqa Island in Fiji, native inhabitants believe that hundreds of years ago, a strong young man discovered a tiny human-like creature trapped in a hole in the river. The man promptly rescued him. In gratitude, the creature taught him to be more powerful than fire. For as long as the sun rose and set, the creature promised, the man and his male descendants would be able to walk on coals.

Today, islanders believe that descendants of that young man live in five local villages. To perform their feat, they dig a chest-high pit in the earth, two to three body-lengths long. While the fire-walkers segregate themselves, avoiding contact with women and abstaining from any food containing coconut, other villagers line the entire pit with round river stones and build a huge log bonfire overtop. Then, just moments before the fire-walkers arrive, they clear the logs to reveal the red-hot stones beneath. The heat is so intense that a thin piece of cloth tossed into the pit will burst into flames.

In silence, the fire-walkers emerge from their seclusion, trot single-file to the pit, and walk quickly onto the stones. They leave the pit with no blisters, no marks, no signs of burns, assuring them that they have achieved the grace of the gods and the protection offered by intense spirituality.

Fire-walkers have practiced their arts in all regions of the world, from Greece to Sri Lanka. And so have spiritualists, psychics, and magicians who have claimed they were immune to the effects of flames. In the 1800s, a Scottish-born

Cold Drink, Anyone?

Between the late 1940s and early 1970s, researchers with the U.S. Air Force and the University of California tested how well people could function and think in rooms heated up to 113°C (235°F). They found that for several minutes, the human body could work as its own refrigerator, staying up to 38°C (100°F) cooler than the heated air.

American named Daniel Douglas Home declared he could communicate with spirits. His powers included lifting furniture off the floor, levitating, and handling flames without burning himself. He could even pick up red-hot coals or tools from the fireplace, all without harm. And though many observers tried to discredit his "tricks," no one succeeded.

There are two possible scientific explanations for these sorts of phenomena. The first is that even though coals can be as hot as 650°C (1200°F), a thin layer of moisture on the soles of the feet or the palms of the hands acts as a barrier between the heat and the skin and protects the fire-walkers or handlers from harm. The second theory is that while the coals or stones are very hot, they are also very small, and small surfaces don't actually give off high levels of heat.

But people who have witnessed fire-walking doubt both these explanations. Occasionally, fire-walkers who seem to lose focus or concentration are actually burned. Why would this be the case, if their feet were protected by water or if the coals weren't giving off high levels of heat?

Those who believe in the spiritual side of fire-walking say that the fire-walkers have risen above the power of fire. Their faith in their abilities or in the protection of their gods is so strong that it allows them to achieve a higher mental and physical state—a state stronger than the hottest flame.

In Christianity, some people believed to be graced by God have also found power to withstand fire. According to the book of Daniel in the Bible, a king named Nebuchadnezzor once commissioned a huge golden statue of himself. But three of his top-ranking officials—Shadrach, Meshack, and Abednego—refused to bow to the statue. They were determined to remain faithful only to God. Nebuchadnezzor was furious and had them thrown into a giant furnace so hot that the men who threw them in died from the heat. There was no way to survive such a place, and yet, Nebuchadnezzor peered into the furnace door and saw four men walking in the flames—the three officials and an angel sent to protect them.

Faced with this evidence of God's power, Nebuchadnezzor changed his ways and restored his advisors to their positions.

Even outside the Bible, there are stories of the Christian God protecting people from the power of fire. At the dawn of the 18th century, thousands of Protestants known as Huguenots looked for safety in the mountains of southern France. After decades of persecution under Catholic French kings, they were determined to fight for the right to practice their religion. According to accounts of the time, one of the Huguenot leaders was a prophet named Pierre Claris. To inspire his followers, he stood at the top of a burning pyre and addressed the crowd, urging them to continue the fight. Then, as 600 astounded people watched, he stepped uninjured from the blaze.

In the mid-1800s, a doctor witnessed a young French nun offering a public prayer to the Virgin Mary. As she sat deep in meditation, the candle in her hands burned lower and lower until the flames flickered over the nun's skin. For 15 minutes, she continued praying, feeling nothing. The doctor examined her shortly after, and found no marks from the flames. The young nun is now known as Saint Bernadette, patron of the sick and the poor.

To spiritualists or fire-walkers or believers in religious miracles, fire seems extraordinary, with mystical authority. But what these believers are actually recognizing is fire's real, physical power. In our day-to-day world, it actually *can* burn away old growth to prepare for new, or grow out of control and destroy property and take lives. For thousands of years, the world's religions have recognized this power and given it symbolic meaning.

In the supernatural world, just as in nature, fire serves a dual role. It can cleanse and purify, or torment and punish. It can prove the presence of gods or the faith of saints, or it can burn the dead in a world of torture.

THREE

Furnace and Forge

FIRE AND INDUSTRY

A flying serpent who breathed flame, Svarog was the most powerful god in the universe for early eastern Europeans. Fire was sacred to him. He used it to melt and form metal, and held it in such respect that he would punish people who swore or spit while trying to kindle a spark.

Svarog was also determined to punish other gods who used fire indiscriminately. The worst of these was Zmey, a multi-headed dragon who traveled the universe killing people for no reason and destroying homes and forests.

Pulling his blacksmith's tongs from his forge, Svarog reached out and plucked Zmey from the sky. Then, with the dragon captured between the pincers, he used the creature to plow a giant furrow, separating the world of the living from the world of the dead.

When this work was done, he released Zmey to rule over the land of the dead and guard the bridge between the two realms. With order restored to the universe, Svarog returned to his place as god of sun, fire, rain, and sky, using his supreme strength to reign over both the Earth and the heavens.

As soon as ancient people gained control over fire, they began to use it to make things. Like the god Svarog once worshiped by the Slavic people, they believed that this destructive force could also be used to create. At first, it was used only to sear food or harden wooden spears. But soon, people discovered that fire allowed them to create all kinds of new materials.

Many of the earliest humans understood that they could collect lumps of clay from riverbanks, press their fists in to create hollows, and use the rough vessels to carry things. But these peoples were constantly moving with the herds or with the seasons, and lumps of clay were of limited use. It wasn't until about 6000 BCE, when groups began settling in more permanent villages, that they began experimenting more with what we would now call pottery.

In different parts of the world—Japan, Egypt, the Middle East, the island of Crete—artisans discovered that by baking clay, they could create strong and heatproof bowls and goblets. Some archeologists believe they learned this by lining firepits with clay and noticing that when the embers had burned away,

Yum, Mush!

Because boiled food is faster to prepare and easier for children and elderly people to eat, some archeologists believe that ancient populations boomed as they discovered how to make pottery.

the clay was left hard and waterproof. Others believe that people lined baskets with clay to carry water or food. Set beside or in a fire, the lining would have baked and hardened.

Once they understood that baking clay made it more useful, it didn't take long for societies to perfect different methods for "firing." One such method still exists today among the tribes of Nigeria: a fire is built around a clay pot, then covered with grass or dung to keep the heat trapped inside. Other peoples discovered that by building ovens—often clay boxes and arches built over a fire and covered with earth—they could better control the strength and the color of the pottery. However it was learned and perfected, the understanding of pottery made new things possible. Water could be carried and stored more easily and food could be boiled or steamed.

THE FIERY FORGE

As some humans were learning to use pottery, others were learning the intricacies of metal. As people began to mine and use copper, iron, and other minerals between 12,000 and 6000 BCE, they searched for ways to mold these materials into tools and weapons. When they found that metal held in the embers of a very hot fire became red and malleable, the art of forging was born.

In Sinai, Egypt, archeologists have found remains of a waist-deep hole in the ground lined with stone. Two holes in the stone would have allowed air to be blown in through pipes to feed a fire. In this makeshift furnace, the archeologists believe that ancient Egyptian artisans placed a small amount of copper ore and charcoal over searing hot embers and managed to achieve temperatures of more than 1000°C (1830°F), allowing them to melt the ore.

In ancient Africa, tribes smelted iron by digging a long trench in the earth. Filling the trench with a carefully mixed and dried combination of ore and charcoal, they would then cover it with a layer of leaves and put a large container on top. Made from the hardened clay of a termite mound and equipped with handles, this container was strong enough to hold a charcoal fire and heat the ore below to more than 1100°C (2000°F). Constantly fanning the fire with hand-powered bellows, workers would drag the container along the trench, so slowly that it would take about four hours to move it across a trench half the height of a man. When they were finished, they would remove the container and the layer of leaves. The ore would have melted and the mineral within it would have bonded to the charcoal to form a purer iron. It cooled into a large block, which could be reheated and shaped into weapons or pots.

In medieval Europe, the process of smelting and forging iron took on an air of mystery. Smiths often set up their shops near their sources of ore, separating themselves from

Gods at Work

In ancient Greece, people believed the steam escaping from the tops of volcanoes was the smoke from the god Vulcan's forge, produced as he crafted weapons for the god of war, Ares, and thunderbolts for the ruler, Zeus.

day-to-day village life. In fact, in ancient France and Spain, entire villages of smiths lived apart from others, opening their doors to sell their products only on special occasions. These smiths—with the power to control fire hot enough to melt metal, then mold that metal into almost any shape—were regarded with awe. They were buried with honor under their anvils, with their tools by their sides.

By about 2500 years ago, the people of Europe and Asia were smelting so much metal that the emissions traveled along air currents all the way to Greenland, where pollutants such as copper drifted to the ice and remained trapped there for modern scientists to discover.

The intense heat used to forge metal or bake clay was turned to other uses as well. In the 15th or 16th century BCE, people in Mesopotamia discovered that silica—found naturally in minerals such as quartz—could be melted into a clear, syrupy fluid. By mixing silica with small amounts of ash or potash, then melting the mixture in a kiln, artisans could create shapes that would harden into glass. By 1500 BCE, Mesopotamians, Phoenicians, and Egyptians were heating glass into long strands and winding the strands into bottles or rounding them into beads. Craftspeople also used saucer-like metal containers or other molds to set glass into final forms. Later, in the first century CE, they learned to blow air through metal pipes to bend the glass into delicate cups and vases with more intricate designs.

In other areas of the world, bakers discovered that the slow heat of an oven could produce entirely new foods. People in coastal regions found they could use fire to evaporate seawater, leaving crystals of salt behind. Others learned that by boiling ashes from their fires with animal fat, they could create soap.

Because of these discoveries, and because of industries such as pottery making, blacksmithing, and glassblowing, societies were constantly changing. With each discovery came inventions and developments. Smelting brought better farm tools, weapons, and building materials. Pottery and glassblowing brought ways for people to express their creativity. And all of these things created new reasons to share ideas with neighboring societies. In parts of the world where trade and industry flourished, civilizations grew steadily more advanced.

Then, after thousands of years of using fire to *make* things, someone discovered a new kind of device—one that used fire to *move* things.

REVOLUTIONARY IDEAS

In the late 1600s, scientists began to experiment with steam. If they used fire to boil water, then kept the resulting steam under pressure, they could use the steam to turn metal blades and actually move a gear. Just as a river turning a water wheel could produce the power to grind wheat, steam churning through a gear could make enough power to run a machine.

In the most common kind of steam engine, engineers boiled water until it evaporated into high-pressure steam. They then released the steam into a metal cylinder. There, the pressure of the steam moved a metal piston—like a hammer—back and forth. The piston rod—like the handle of the hammer—reached out of the cylinder, attached to metal rods, and turned the gears. Power! Suddenly, inventors could turn the energy of fire into the energy of motion, and use it to move weaving looms, water pumps, and eventually even ships and trains.

By the 1700s and 1800s, these fire- and steam-powered engines were changing the world. While workers had once woven cloth by hand at home in their cottages, now they reported to massive factories, where machines produced goods faster. In 1803, a British engineer named Richard Trevithick invented the first steam locomotive and put the horse-drawn cart on the road to extinction. And while these changes may not have seemed directly related to fire, flames were still in the background, creating the steam.

As industry quickly found more uses for the steam engine, scientists were already working on yet another type of combustion. This time, they designed engines that used fire not just to heat water, but to heat gas within the engine itself and move the metal parts.

Potato Power

To understand how powerful combustion must have seemed to early machine-makers, imagine a metal tube, closed at one end. If a drop of gasoline and a potato were placed in the tube, and then the gasoline was lit, the expansion of the gas—like a miniature explosion—would create enough energy to fire the potato the length of one-and-a-half football fields. And all that movement would have come from the energy inside a single drop of gas, lit under pressure.

In this kind of internal combustion engine, a spark was used to ignite a small amount of gas inside a cylinder. The drop of gas released so much energy that air would burst out of the cylinder to move a metal shaft. By constantly adding a little fuel, sparking it, then using the explosion of energy—hundreds of times per minute—scientists created more powerful machines than ever before.

Both steam and internal combustion engines opened new doors for industry. Mining companies could now pump water out of mine shafts, allowing them to dig deeper than ever before. Smelting companies could use gas to power their machines instead of wood or charcoal. Corporations expanded and cities grew—all because of sparks deep inside combustion engines.

While some engineers were working on better engines, others were perfecting the metal smelting and refining processes developed by their ancestors. In the late 1700s, as steam began churning factory engines, most things were being made out of wrought iron. But builders knew that a metal alloy called steel—a mix of iron and a carefully controlled amount of carbon—was much stronger. Unfortunately, steel was phenomenally expensive. To produce a ton, a refinery had to burn three tons of a coal product called coke.

In 1855, English inventor Henry Bessemer created an egg-shaped converter. A pipe in the top allowed metal to be poured in, while small holes in the base allowed air to be blown through. This process of blowing air through molten metal separated iron from other metals, the same way oil and vinegar might separate in a salad dressing bottle. Now, scientists had a way to finely control the amount of carbon in iron. As sparks flew from the converter, they could tip the egg and pour molten steel into molds. This new conversion method was much faster. It still took fire, but it burned half the amount of coke.

Just as Bessemer was perfecting his converter, two 22-year-olds were experimenting with another mineral called alumina. Both Charles Hall of the United States and Paul Heroult of France knew that at high heat—900° C (1650°F)—a chemical reaction could turn alumina into metallic aluminum. But heating alumina to that temperature with a regular fire wasn't practical.

Somehow, working on opposite sides of the Atlantic Ocean, both men made the same discovery: if they poured alumina into a steel container, then ran a massive electrical current through the container, they could create the high temperatures. It was almost as if a bolt of lightning was hitting the minerals. And if they didn't mind using masses of electricity and pouring loads of carbon dioxide into the air as a byproduct, they could cheaply produce aluminum for cans, kitchen utensils, wires, ship propellers, and countless other products.

Together, powerful combustion engines and refined metals gave engineers the power to build cross-continental railways, create stronger, steel-hulled battleships, and cheaply produce guns and cannons. In the United States, where entrepreneurs quickly achieved the world's highest steel production rate, these new technologies meant industry could boom.

The same technologies continue feeding industry today, and fire remains a direct part of many processes. In most cases, the sparks are hidden deep within engines or furnaces . . . but not always. The plumbing pipes in our homes, for example, are still welded together using open flames. In gas welding, acetylene and oxygen are stored in a tank, then pressed through a nozzle where they ignite to produce a hot flame. This flame can melt metal, creating joins in plates or pipes.

Flames are also used to harden the outside edges of steel parts, such as the gears used in our cars. Machinists ignite gas to form a flame and run the metal under the flame, then immediately pour cold water on the surface to cool it down. The interior of the steel remains slightly more flexible, while the exterior is considerable tougher. This is important for parts such as saw blades—the edge of the blade can be strong enough to slice through a tree trunk, but just flexible enough not to shatter if it hits a rock.

Scientists have also developed and refined the steam engines of the 1700s and the internal combustion engines of the 1800s until they can now produce enough energy to blast a rocket into space.

At the Kennedy Space Center in Florida, 408,200 kilograms (900,000 pounds) of liquid oxygen is stored at one edge of the launch area, while the same amount of hydrogen sits at the other end. When a shuttle is ready to launch, the

Blastoff

When NASA launches a shuttle into space, a 152-person fire crew is standing by to respond to emergencies. If necessary, they can help astronauts climb into wire baskets, slide from the launch pad, and escape in armored vehicles.

two gases flow into a divided tank below the rocket. At the last moment, technicians remove the division and ignite the gas, causing the massive explosion necessary to blast the shuttle through the atmosphere. As the flames shoot into the sky, excess heat, smoke, and fire are directed through a massive brick and concrete trench where they can't harm any launch machinery. Meanwhile, thousands of gallons of water are pumped onto the launch pad to contain the flames, prevent sparks, and muffle the overwhelming noise of the launch.

NEW DANGERS

Fire, and its use in machines and engines, had allowed companies all over the world to gather their workers together and produce products faster, more efficiently, and for less money. Yet it also created new dangers. When fuels are lit under the right conditions, they can power everything from welding torches to rockets. When they're lit accidentally, they put the environment and people in serious danger.

In the earliest factories, workers crowded together at trestle tables were easily trapped by flames, and businesses and homes squeezed together on city streets could pass sparks from one roof to another. The industrial revolution made booming cities more vulnerable to flames than ever before. In 1666, sparks in a London bakery spread through ramshackle row houses so quickly that most of the city went up in smoke. In 1871, a fire in the wood-processing center of Peshtigo, Wisconsin, tore through forests, towns, and city blocks, killing more than 1000 people.

From garment factories to offshore oil rigs, each new industry brought its own fire hazards. In the 1980s, an oil company in the North Sea was producing 300,000 barrels a day from the underwater Piper Oilfield. The largest platform, floating on 114 meters (474 feet) of water and housing 240 crew members, was Piper Alpha.

On July 6, 1988, the crew was at work all over the platform. A new pipeline had just been completed, causing a few minor complications, and a pressure relief valve from one of the gas compressors was removed for repair. Underwater, divers had shut off the automatic firefighting systems as they checked the massive pumps for any problems. Then, as night fell, the missing pressure relief valve allowed invisible, odorless gas to burst through part of the machine and spread across the platform. With only a single, random spark from equipment, the gas ignited.

Fed by the flowing oil, the blaze soon spread over the platform, melting the firewalls in its path and blazing its way into the crew quarters. A very few men managed to leap into the crashing waves of the North Sea and survive until rescue boats or helicopters could find them; 167 died.

Faced with storm winds and seven-story waves, the company called in the world's most famous firefighter, Red Adair, to douse the blaze. From aboard a firefighting ship which he had designed himself, the blustering Texan and his crew sent 270,000 liters (70,000 gallons) of water per minute onto the machinery, eventually cooling the metal and removing enough debris that men could access the platform itself and cap the pipelines. The fire took three weeks to douse.

THE INDUSTRY OF FIRE FIGHTING

Red Adair's success on the North Sea points to another major change that occurred when combustion combined with human industry: methods of fire fighting transformed from lines of people with buckets and hoses to trained crews with highly specialized equipment.

Firefighters have existed for centuries. In 24 CE, the Roman emperor Augustus created a crew of watchmen whose job was to comb the city for signs of fire and sound the alarm if needed. When flames were spotted, citizens would quickly help fill and carry buckets of water to douse the blaze, knowing their own homes and businesses were at stake.

Methods didn't change much until the Great Fire of London in 1666. After that, private insurance companies took charge of training crews and arranging for hand pumps to throw more water at sudden blazes. It wasn't until 1830 in Edinburgh, Scotland, that the modern fire department was founded, with standard firefighting procedures and safety training for workers. London followed suit in 1865.

The first superintendent of London's newborn fire brigade was Sir Eyre Massey-Shaw, a former army officer who had the following views on fire fighting:

"A fireman, to be successful, must enter buildings. He must get in below, above, on every side; from opposite houses, over back walls, over side walls, through panels of doors, through windows, through skylights, through holes cut by himself in gates, walls and the roof. He must know how to reach the attic from the basement by ladders placed on half-burnt stairs, and the basement from the attic by a rope made fast on a chimney. His whole success depends on his getting in and remaining there . . ."

But despite the value he placed on the agility and courage of his crews, Massey-Shaw was also a man who saw the value of equipment. He had brass helmets made for his workers, ordered more steam engines to help pump water, increased the number of fire stations, and had telegraph lines strung to connect those stations. In the 1600s and 1700s, firefighters had dug down to city pipes and punctured them to access water, but by Sir Eyre's time, many towns and cities were already equipping their streets with hydrants like the ones we have today.

In the early 1900s, the invention of the internal combustion engine meant that firefighters could now rely on mechanical fire engines rather than horse-drawn wagons. Their vehicles were equipped with two motors—one to propel the vehicle, and the other to power the water pump. In 1907, the year before Sir Eyre's death, firefighters began using the first fire engine with a motor that ran both the vehicle and the pump.

Soon, firefighting vehicles were also carrying water reservoirs, huge lengths of hose, and extendable ladders. Along with the axes and hammers used in Sir Eyre's day, firefighters could choose from an array of power saws and jacks. And new fire-resistant fabric and self-contained breathing equipment protected the workers.

Today, firefighters don heat-resistant gloves and boots. They wear helmets specially designed to withstand heat and impact on top of fabric hoods embedded with fire-resistant carbon. In their trucks, they carry everything from axes and bolt cutters to saws and even portable generators—all the tools they might need to gain access to the source of the flames.

They are also well versed in the science behind fires. They understand the fire pyramid (fuel, heat, oxygen, and chemical reactions) and can assess each blaze to decide which wall of the pyramid will be the easiest to remove. Should they shut the gas valves, removing the fuel, or flood the building with water, eliminating the heat? Each fire requires a different response. To decide, crews rely on both instinct and science. They might assess the shape and color of the flames, the color of the smoke, and the way the smoke seems to be forced from the building. If they know what's stored inside the building, they can predict the amount of fuel a fire has left to burn, and estimate the danger of explosion.

Thanks to trained firefighters and high-tech prevention, most of us feel relatively safe from fire in day-to-day life. We have wired our homes and businesses with fire alarms and sprinkler systems, and placed our professional firefighters on constant call. We space our buildings farther apart and ensure our factories meet safety regulations. We have almost forgotten that our workplaces can be destroyed by flames, or that our cities were built because of fire-driven industries.

Since the days when craftspeople built bonfires to heat kilns or burned charcoal to smelt ore, people have been using fire to change the world around them. Today our fuels are more efficient and our fires are hidden inside engine hoods or furnaces, but they're still present, simmering within our homes and cars and flickering at the edges of our awareness.

Pump It Up!

The hoses and nozzles used by modern city fire departments can send water jetting into a building at the rate of 380 liters (100 gallons) per minute.

FOUR

Where There's Smoke . . .

FIRE AND COMMUNICATION

Fox knew how to speak to other foxes, but he yearned to communicate with the other types of animals. He began by imitating the cry of the geese.

Amused by his efforts, the geese decided they would allow fox to fly with them. He could practice his cry as they flew. Giving fox a pair of wings, they lifted him into the air. But they made him promise never to open his eyes while in flight.

Fox promised, and soared with the geese, trying out their cry and proud of his ability to speak with these new friends. The geese flew over fields, lakes, and mountains, then low over a settlement of fireflies.

Startled by the sudden brightness, fox opened his eyes. And fell headlong into the midst of the fireflies. He found himself in a village surrounded by a high wall and populated by glowing creatures. In the center of the settlement burned a bright fire, something fox had never seen before.

Always eager to seize new opportunities, fox learned to speak the light- and flame-based language used by the fireflies. Then he began to think about what a difference fire would make to his friends outside the walls. Determined to capture part of the flames, he tied a piece of cedar bark to his tail, then offered to dance for the fireflies.

As his audience cheered for his performance, fox "accidentally" stepped too close to the fire. The bark on his tail caught fire. Running headlong through the village, fox called out to a cedar tree, "Bend down and catapult me over the wall."

Soon, fox had escaped the village and was sprinting through the fields, his tail scattering sparks as he went. He ran all the way to his burrow before the fireflies caught up with him and took his fire away forever.

But even though fox had lost his flames, he had left sparks sprinkled throughout the world. The Apache people were able to gather these sparks, and soon learned to use fire to light their camps and cook their food.

BURNING BEACONS

Like the fox of the Apache legend, many people of the ancient world longed for easier ways to communicate. When enemies attacked, there were no emergency telephone numbers to call for help. There was no simple way to send for reinforcements or warn other villages that danger was coming.

But on the other side of the world, in ancient Greece, people had found a creative way to send signals over long distances using huge bonfires. Some historians believe that when the city of Troy fell to enemy forces, a series of fire signals was lit. Within three nights, the news traveled from bonfire to bonfire, north and west along the Aegean Sea from what is now Turkey to the shores of Greece, until officials in Athens learned of the defeat.

In the second century BCE, a Greek historian named

Polybius wrote about fire signals in *The Histories*. He talked about how useful fire signals were in war—when warned of an approaching attack or a recent defeat, forces stationed several days away could react quickly. But Polybius also wrote about the disadvantages of fire. Both the sender and the receiver had to know a prearranged code for each message. For example, they would have had to agree in the weeks before the battle that two fires meant defeat, and three meant victory. While this was okay for basic messages, it left no room for change. What if the sender had detected a traitor or spy, and needed to let the receiver know? Polybius suggested a new system using 10 torches. By lighting the torches in various patterns, the sender could create 25 characters with different meanings. In essence, Polybius was creating a kind of alphabet with torchlight.

Historians today don't know how often Polybius's system was used, and they don't know if such elaborate systems existed elsewhere. But they do know that fire signals were common in several other countries, including Korea. Seven hundred years ago, when lookouts along the Korean coast spotted Japanese ships on the horizon, they quickly sounded the alarm: raiders approaching! The guards woke their companions and ran to light signal fires. Ten minutes later, massive rock structures that rose like beehives along the walls of the fortification blazed with light.

From the nearby countryside, farmers and laborers poured into the fort, seeking refuge from the raiders. And a few hours away, soldiers at the next station were lighting their own fires, signaling to the west. One after another, signal fires were lit from fort to fort, until news of the raid reached the capital city and the eyes of King Taejo himself.

As he gained control of Korea in the 1300s, King Taejo reinforced and added to the system of fire signal stations throughout the country. Many of the bases had already existed for 200 years, part of an elaborate system of communication that allowed the army to quickly respond to threats anywhere in the land. From the farthest reaches of the coastline, fires at any of 673 beacon stations could be lit in sequence, and the flames visible at night or the smoke seen during the day could take simple codes—perhaps the size or timing of an imminent attack—over 250 kilometers (155 miles) to the capital in less than 12 hours. If the king himself was in danger or enemies threatened the capital, fires would blaze in five massive stone kilns on the hillside that formed the southern border of the city. The flames there could send messages even to the most scattered parts of the army.

China was another nation that used a system of fire signals. In the 1500s, as China's Ming Dynasty struggled to protect its borders against Mongol invaders, the general in charge constantly ran into the same difficulty. With his limited forces, he had to protect a border that extended for many days' journey in both directions. But on the other side of the border walls, the Mongols could meet and choose a single point of attack. The Chinese defenders, spread out

Old Flames

The capital city of King Taejo's time is now Seoul, Korea. Its stone kilns have survived more than seven centuries to become a protected monument in Namsan Park.

among many posts, could never respond quickly enough. Again and again, their bases were overrun.

The general solved the problem by building massive signal towers at each of his forts. Using smoke in daytime and blazing fires at night, soldiers could signal for help when Mongols attacked. Once the troops in nearby forts knew of the danger, they could rush to assist. By the 1580s, there were more than 800 towers along the border. Signals could be passed from one tower to another until they traveled more than 965 kilometers (600 miles) per day, limited only by the time it took to build new blazes at each station.

Many Native groups in North America also used smoke and fire to communicate, long before Europeans arrived in North America. From a hillside, a puff of smoke could be seen for great distances. Using a blanket to alternately fan and smother a fire, people could make sequences of smoke puffs, communicating with other parties.

Usually, these smoke signals weren't used with formal codes or systems. Codes could be known or interpreted by enemies, always nearby. Instead, families or friends would prearrange signals—one puff means we've arrived, two puffs means we're safe. But some tribes, such as the Apaches, did use more complicated forms of code—rows of fire where the number of smoke columns and the size of each column might mean specific things. At night, some people used flaming arrows shot into the air to send messages. In that case, messages could be sent according to the number of arrows used, the distance between them, and the shapes they formed as they flew. A line where each arrow flew higher than the last might mean one thing, while a perfectly horizontal line might mean another.

Sometimes, it doesn't take a system of beacons or an elaborate code to communicate with fire. In Boston in 1775, leaders such as John Hancock and Samuel Adams began stirring Americans to rebel against British rule. The British decided to stop any rebellion before it began, and one of the first steps was to destroy American weapons and arrest Hancock and Adams.

Knowing that troops from Boston were likely to either march or sail to Lexington to capture the leaders, a silversmith-turned-messenger named Paul Revere came up with a plan. He instructed a friend to watch for the movement of the troops. If they left by land, the friend was to hang one lantern in the tower of a local church. If they left by sea, he was told to hang two lanterns.

According to a story that has now become a legendary part of United States history, Revere waited across the river in Charlestown until he saw two lights. Then he and his horse flew through the countryside, stopping at each farm and village along the way to shout a warning. He arrived in Lexington

S.O.S.

A few smoke signals have survived to this day. Scouting organizations in Canada and the United States use three puffs of smoke to signal danger. And hikers lost in the woods can still light three side-by-side fires to tell passing planes that they're in trouble.

before the British did, and was able to warn Adams and Hancock. Thanks to his prearranged fire signal, the people of Massachusetts were armed and ready to respond when the British arrived, and the first battle of the American Revolution began.

BEACONS IN THE NIGHT

Long before Asian armies were signaling with fire, and probably even before the Native peoples of North America were signaling with smoke, a ruler in the Mediterranean decided to use fire as a guide and a warning to incoming ships.

In 290 BCE, the Egyptian king Ptolemy I ruled over Alexandria, one of the busiest port cities in the world. As trade increased, ships arrived in his harbor at all hours of the day and night, bringing spices, cloth, and wine and carrying away papyrus, medicine, jewelry, and perfume. But in a time long before radio or radar beams, it was sometimes hard to see a port at night, let alone navigate around bluffs and sandbars to the harbor entrance.

To guide arrivals, Ptolemy decided to build a monument to himself and to the city. He authorized the construction of a massive beacon at the entrance to the harbor, and hired one of the most famous artisans of the day—Greek architect Sostratus of Cnidos.

Two decades later, when the emperor's son, Ptolemy II, ruled the city, Sostratus completed his masterpiece. The Pharos of Alexandria, the largest lighthouse in the ancient world, rose 122 meters (400 feet) into the air in a series of steps and spirals, with another small tower perched on top of the first to hold a massive basket of fire. Each day, huge quantities of wood were hauled up the spiraling steps by hundreds of slaves, to keep the beacon burning each night.

And from 50 kilometers (30 miles) away, mariners could see the welcoming glow.

According to histories of the time, Ptolemy II ordered that only one thing be inscribed on the tower: "Ptolemy." Angry that his own name wouldn't mark the tower, Sostratus secretly made his own engraving in the stone: "Sostratus son of Dexiphanes of Knidos on behalf of all mariners to the savior gods." He then covered his etched words with a thick layer of plaster, and inscribed "Ptolemy" on the plaster. Over several decades, rain and weather wore the plaster away, revealing the stone inscription underneath.

While the Pharos of Alexandria was the most impressive of its time, it wasn't the first lighthouse built along the shores of the Mediterranean. Since as early as 600 BCE, a lighthouse had guided sailors along the Dardanelles Strait between the Black Sea and the Mediterranean. The entrance to Athens was said to be marked by fire beacons at night, and

Lighthouse Legacy

The Pharos of Alexandria is known as one of the seven wonders of the ancient world. After more than 1500 years of use, the beacon was destroyed by earthquakes in the 1400s. Divers exploring the harbor floor found remains of the structure in 1994.

the Romans built lighthouses in Italy, Spain, France, and even on the shores of England. In Dover, on the English coast at the point nearest France, two lighthouses were built by the Romans. Only the foundations of one remain, but the other is 12 meters (40 feet) high, and stands perched on a clifftop more than 100 meters (330 feet) above the waves. A bonfire lit at the top could be spotted from France.

With the end of the Roman Empire in 476 CE, the Dark Ages began—a time of little learning and few accomplishments in Europe. And the Dark Ages were literally dark, as well. Almost all the Roman lighthouses fell into ruin. After all, a beacon could guide enemies into a harbor as well as traders. It could provide light to smugglers and criminals operating by night. And, by preventing shipwrecks, it could eliminate the valuable trade goods that washed up on shore from doomed vessels.

It wasn't until the 1500s that traders and local harbor masters began to once again see the value of beacons. One of the first was an English lord named William Marshall, a man developing a trading port at New Ross on the southeast shore of Ireland. The harbor lay along a treacherous shoreline, and to ensure ships could safely navigate, he paid a local monastery to build and maintain a lighthouse. Using local limestone, the monks constructed a tower 25 meters (82 feet) high, with walls 3.5 meters (11 feet) thick at the base. The monks tended the light for 400 years, and supervised the replacement of the open bonfire in the metal basket at the peak with an oil lantern in the 1600s. The lighthouse is still in use today.

By the early 1700s, lighthouses were once again in use around the world. The first beacon in the United States was built on Little Brewster Island at the entrance to Boston Harbor in 1716. Like others of its time, it used a glazed lantern and a candle chandelier to produce enough light to guide incoming ships. In Canada, the first lighthouse was built in 1733 in Louisburg, Nova Scotia, a 20-meter (66-foot) tower with oil-fed flames in the wooden chamber on top. When the wooden chamber was accidentally set alight one night and destroyed in 1737—a common occurrence in early lighthouses—it was rebuilt in brick and stone.

In the late 1800s, lighthouses remained remote outposts, often perched on stormy coastlines hours from the nearest settlements. In maritime emergencies, they were sometimes the only places of refuge available. One such emergency occurred on October 26, 1890, outside the harbor of Cleveland, Ohio. Threatened by storm winds and heavy waves, a steamer was forced to cut its tow ropes to enter the harbor, leaving a large barge with eight crew members anchored outside the breakwater, the huge stone wall that helped protect the port. After tugboats from inside the harbor tried and failed to attach new ropes, the barge careened against the breakwater and disintegrated, leaving the sailors fighting for their lives.

Having watched the disaster unfold from the harbor lighthouse, lighthouse keeper Frederick Hatch wrapped himself against the storm and set out onto the breakwater itself, braving the waves that crashed over the stones. He found several people trying to climb from the water and helped them back along the breakwater to the lighthouse. Then, when he couldn't reach through the waves and grasp the other people he could see in the water, Hatch took a small boat into the shadow of the breakwater and pulled in a sailor and the captain's wife. He turned toward shore, but a sudden wave washed over the boat and threw all three of them into the water. Luckily, Hatch had tied the boat to the lighthouse tower and was able to grab the rope, pulling himself and the woman to shore.

The other sailor and several others were later rescued by a local lifesaving crew. When morning broke and the storm abated, the lifesaving crew and the lighthouse keeper were able to communicate once more. They found they had rescued seven crew members. Only a single sailor had drowned.

FLOATING LIGHTS

Even under the brave and watchful eyes of lighthouse keepers like Hatch, travel at sea remained hard and hazardous. A lighthouse might mark a dangerous point or a harbor entrance, but shifting sandbars and treacherous reefs just offshore could still easily wreck a wooden ship. And yet, how could a lighthouse be built on a constantly changing sandbar?

In 1728, a group of London merchants tired of losing ships to the Nore Sands in the estuary of the Thames River gathered and proposed a floating lighthouse—a ship anchored on the sands with fires burning on the mast to warn other ships away. In 1730, the government agreed to the proposal and converted a small trading vessel. A long crossbar was hung on the mast, with oil lanterns at each end. With ropes, the crew could lower the crossbar to the deck, refuel the lanterns, and hoist them into the air again.

For the sailors who worked on board the new lightship, life was difficult and dangerous. They lived on deck with little shelter during storms. When rain pounded down or winds whipped up the waves, it was almost impossible to keep the lanterns on the crossbar lit. And several times, during particularly violent storms, the anchor chains broke and the ship was sent lurching into the open ocean. Still, the number of shipwrecks decreased and London merchants declared the lightship a success.

By the early 1800s, North America adopted lightships as well. The first ones guided ships safely into Chesapeake Bay in Virginia and proved so helpful that by 1909, 56 ships were posted at various points off the coast. A few decades later, however, technology had improved enough that floating buoys could usually take their places.

PYROTECHNIC S.O.S.

A sizzle of magnesium and a brilliant burst of light—that's what happens when soldiers, lost hikers, or rescue workers light emergency flares. In the modern world, they're most useful in places where there's no other artificial light. A soldier in the desert might set off a flare to show a plane where to best drop supplies; a submarine might launch one to illuminate the depths of the sea; a search plane in the uninhabited Arctic might drop one to blaze over the ice.

On October 31, 1991, search and rescue technician Arnold Macauley flew with his Nova Scotia–based crew through a relentless blizzard at the northern tip of Ellesmere Island. They were aboard a Hercules transport plane, searching the ice below for another Hercules that had crashed the day before. Again and again, the crew shot flares onto the ice, the light reflecting against the clouds and snow to show only more clouds and more snow. For hours, the plane flew a search pattern as the crew dropped more than a hundred flares. Then, at last, there was a flash of metal as they caught a glimpse of wreckage.

From 300 meters (1000 feet) in the air, Macauley and five other technicians parachuted through the storm toward the blaze of their most recently dropped flare. When they landed—safely—they found 13 of the crashed plane's 18 original passengers. After receiving basic first aid, the survivors were lifted off the ice and into the plane, once again guided by flares.

Lighthouses and lightships changed forever in the mid-1900s. In lighthouses, more elaborate lenses focused light and sent it farther out to sea; electric lamps replaced open flames and oil lanterns; eventually, computers replaced the lighthouse keepers themselves. In the same way, optical telegraphs—electric lights flashed from station to station—replaced smoke and fire signals for sending messages. The optical telegraphs themselves were then replaced by telegraphs and telephone lines.

Now, in an age where computers bring instant information from all corners of the globe, it's surprising to discover that fire signals are still in use. But boaters carry flares and orange smoke signals to send into the sky in case of emergency, and police officers and emergency vehicles carry highway flares to warn motorists of accidents. They're relatively inexpensive, they're easy to carry, and they instantly signal danger on a dark night.

To search and rescue technicians like the ones who scanned the Arctic ice, or to paramedics aiding accident victims on a winding mountain road, a fire signal isn't an artifact of the past. And in the midst of a nighttime emergency, it probably isn't difficult to imagine a time when fire was the world's best and fastest form of communication.

FIVE

All Fired Up

FIRE AND EMOTION

Sati was the daughter of the Hindu king Daksha, a proud and powerful man. When Sati met and fell in love with Shiva, the god of destruction, her father was horrified. Shiva consorted with demons and spirits—he wasn't a suitable match for a young and beautiful girl. But Sati was stubborn and love-struck. She married Shiva against her father's wishes, and left her home to live with the god.

Furious, Daksha planned a huge banquet, inviting every-one he knew, but intentionally leaving Shiva out of the festiv-ities. Hoping to mend her relationship with her father, Sati attended the banquet anyway. But while she was there, the king was so insulting toward Shiva that Sati grew more and more angry. How could her father speak of her husband this way? Devoted to Shiva and not knowing how else to defend his reputation, she threw herself into the fire in protest.

When he heard about his wife's death, Shiva went wild with grief. He cut off two locks of his hair and threw them to the ground, where they grew into the demons Veerabhadhra and MahaKali. These terrifying creations descended upon the banquet and slaughtered Daksha, along with many of his guests. But the gods Vishnu and Bhrama took pity on the king and begged Shiva to reconsider. Shiva brought the man back to life—after replacing his head with the head of a goat.

The devoted Sati was eventually reborn as Parvati, and once again married Shiva. This time, she remained with him forever.

THE POWER OF LOVE

What makes us flush when the girl or boy of our dreams walks by? Why do we refer to the heat of passion, or say we're burning with desire?

In scientific terms, when we feel a physical attraction to someone, we breathe faster, our heart rate increases, and blood flows more quickly through our bodies. When humans are "hot and bothered," we actually *are* hot. But our association of love and fire goes far beyond feeling a little warm when prince or princess charming walks by. Hundreds of Hollywood movies have shown characters falling in love in front of crackling fireplaces. Pop stars have sung to us about smoldering eyes, burning love, and hearts on fire. And every romance novel seems to include a candlelit love scene. So is it true that fire can actually "spark" romance?

According to proponents of feng shui, a system of positioning objects based on ancient Chinese beliefs, the world is divided into the five elements of water, wood, fire, earth, and metal. Because fire is most closely associated with love and romance, candles in the bedroom can bring new heat to a relationship. And a pair of candles can even help someone single invite a second person into his or her life.

The link between feng shui and candles might be new to many Westerners, but the connection between fire and romance runs deeply through another Chinese tradition. On the 15th day of the lunar year, people in China and Korea celebrate the Lantern Festival by taking to the streets with elaborate paper lamps. As well as a general time of joy and playfulness, this is a traditional time for matchmaking. In past generations, upper-class women who spent most of their lives indoors would emerge onto the streets, possibly to be spotted by eligible men. Professional matchmakers hurried through the towns weighing horoscopes and destinies. Even today, parents might give their children more freedom during the evening festivities of the Lantern Festival, in hopes they will find love.

Other cultures also include flames in their celebrations of romance. At a Jewish wedding ceremony, fire represents light and joy. When the escorts—usually the parents—of the bride and groom walk down the aisle, they carry candles as symbols of the happiness that is to come. In a traditional Hindu wedding ceremony, an actual fire is lit under a canopy. It brings light and knowledge to the bride and groom as

Love Moves the World

Empedocles, the same Greek philosopher who argued that our bodies were made up of the four elements of earth, air, water, and fire, also said that these elements mingled with two forces—love and strife—to cause all motion in the universe.

well as happiness. It also serves as a witness to the marriage, as if the Hindu fire god Agni were present in the flames.

BURNING FOR LOVE?

Along with the spark of new romance, flames can also represent extreme emotion. One of the most radical ties between love and fire lies in the Hindu practice of *sati,* a tradition that involves a widow throwing herself on the funeral pyre of her husband and killing herself, just as the mythical Sati did in the tale of Sati and Shiva. *Sati* has existed in parts of India for more than 2000 years and when British authorities attempted to track the number of sati widows in the 1800s, they estimated that about 600 women each year were killing themselves in this manner.

Although much more rare now, the practice hasn't entirely ended. In 1987, an 18-year-old woman named Roop Kanwar made international headlines when she died in the flames of her husband's funeral. Roop had been married for eight months when her 24-year-old husband died suddenly. On September 4, in the city of Deorala in northwestern India, she dressed herself in her wedding gown, climbed the young man's funeral pyre, cradled his head in her lap, and died in the flames.

The event immediately sparked rumors and arguments across India. How did such a young man die? Was it appendicitis, as the family claimed, or had he poisoned himself after failing his medical school admission exams? Had Roop climbed the pyre voluntarily, after studying the traditional practice of sati, or had she been drugged by her in-laws? Had she fallen from the pyre and been helped back in, or had she tried to escape and been pushed back in?

Despite hundreds of witnesses, no clear story emerged.

And while several members of the family were arrested for participating in the event, no one was ever charged.

To feminists and many modern Hindus, the event was a tragedy. They believed that the practice of sati allowed families to force women to their deaths, and took advantage of the grief-stricken mental states of young women.

But to Hindus who believed in the practice of sati, Roop's sacrifice transformed her into a goddess called a *satimata*. When her husband died so young, traditional Hindu women might have believed it was a failure on Roop's part to care for him as she should have. But by throwing herself onto his funeral pyre, she proved that her feelings were strong and pure. She had made the ultimate sacrifice for love.

Not all connections between fire, love, and death have the violent nature of sati. In Japan, Buddhists believe that on one night each summer, the doors of the afterworld open and the spirits of beloved ancestors can temporarily travel back to their homes. To guide these spirits, people light elaborate lanterns in their windows. Inside, sweet cakes, rice, and flowers await as offerings to the dead.

Banning the Blaze

Several Indian rulers in the 16th and 17th centuries attempted to stop the practice of sati. British colonists banned it in the 1800s, and the last Indian state to allow it declared sati illegal in 1846.

At the end of the evening festivities, people flock to the edges of their local rivers or the shores of the ocean and light tiny candles on floating lanterns. As they drift away on the water, these lanterns guide the spirits back to the afterworld, where they will wait another year.

BLISTERING HATE

Under the canopy of a wedding celebration or in lanterns that guide the spirits of ancestors, flames represent love. Yet they can also serve as a powerful symbol of hate.

In the 1920s, a group of American white supremacists called the Ku Klux Klan, or KKK, rose to such power that it claimed more than 100,000 official members. These extremist Protestant Christians believed that white people were naturally superior, and that society's problems were caused by Jewish people, black people, immigrants, and Catholics. Any difficulty in finding a job, for example, could easily be blamed on competition from minority groups.

Ku Klux Klan members went to great lengths to harass and terrorize their targets, and one of their most frightening symbols was a burning cross. Dressed entirely in white, with hoods over their heads, men would gather on the lawn outside someone's home, erect a giant cross, and light it on fire in the middle of the night, often chanting racial slurs, vandalizing property, and threatening the lives of those inside.

Members of the KKK insisted that they weren't burning the cross as a symbol of sacrilege, but rather illuminating it as a sign of their powerful beliefs. And they argued that their rights to freedom of speech and religion should protect their activities. But in 2003, the United States Supreme Court ruled that although burning a cross as a sign of shared ideas was okay, burning a cross with the intent to intimidate others could be viewed as a hate crime.

By the 1930s, membership in the KKK had begun to decline. But on the other side of the world, supporters of another extremist group were turning to fire to emphasize their own beliefs. In 1933, inspired by a hate-filled speech by a Nazi party organizer, young people and students in 34 cities tore books by Jewish and other "un-German" authors off library shelves and used them to build enormous bonfires in the streets. In their minds, they were using fire to purify German literature of works by undesirable authors.

Library Logic

According to one story of the destruction of the Great Library of Alexandria in Egypt, ruler Caliph Omar was responsible for a mass burning of books. Sometime between 581 and 644, he decided that God was about to destroy the world. He had every book in the library burned, arguing that books opposing the existence of God should be destroyed, and those supporting the existence of God were obviously no longer needed.

The Nazis weren't the first to burn books to rid the world of opposing viewpoints. In the second century BCE, Shi Tuang Ti became the first emperor to unite China, discarding the old feudal system and imposing a new government, new laws and punishments, and a new standard system of writing. To ensure his philosophies and his version of history survived after his death, Shi Tuang Ti had 460 opposing scholars buried alive. He then burned every book in his kingdom, keeping only one copy of each for his own personal library. And his personal library was burned upon his death.

Nazis may have claimed their book burnings were meant to cleanse, and KKK members might have claimed their burning crosses were simply religious symbols, but their actions sparked the same response as Shi Tuang Ti's burning of books: fear.

We all feel some measure of fear and awe when we see a house or forest fire. This helps to keep us safe. It ensures we maintain a healthy respect for things such as matches and lighters, knowing how easily flames can grow out of control and threaten our lives or consume our possessions.

Fire-Phobes

There are a few people who suffer from what doctors label an "unhealthy" fear of fire. People with this sort of pyrophobia are terrified of flames and think they are constantly in danger of being burned.

Yet even this small amount of fear leaves us open to manipulation. By burning a book or a cross, groups such as the ones mentioned above are sending a message: "Scared? Then stay out our way. Obey our rules." They use fire as a way to gain control and power over others.

FIRE-SETTERS

It's not only extremist groups who use fire to spark fear and draw power; individuals can turn flames to their own uses as well. Arsonists, for example, are often motivated by anger or revenge. Some researchers suggest that up to half of all arson fires are started by people seeking revenge. These fire-setters are usually male, with below-average intelligence and education. Their girlfriends have broken up with them, their bosses have fired them, or their parents have punished them. Determined to take control, to prove that they are more powerful, they set homes or properties on fire.

Perhaps even more frightening are the arsonists who *aren't* motivated by revenge. A small number of fire-setters—about 10 percent—love the thrill and the feelings of power and control they gain by starting a fire and watching it grow. These people don't need anger or revenge to spur their actions. They simply need an opportunity.

In southern California in the 1980s, arson investigators began to suspect that one man was responsible for a series of fires—and they began to suspect that the criminal was one of their colleagues. The device used to spark the blazes was a simple arrangement of matches and a fuse, difficult to trace. But the fires seemed to be set in the vicinity of arson conferences around the region. After a single fingerprint was found at one of the crime scenes, police began tracking a man named John Leonard Orr, a fire investigator with the Glendale Fire

Department. He was arrested in 1991 and sentenced to life in prison.

Orr seems to have taken pride in secretly setting fires and in outwitting his fellow investigators for so long. Some people believe that a book he wrote about a serial arsonist is actually an autobiography.

Unlike Orr, most arsonists are never caught. It's often difficult even to confirm arson as a cause of a blaze. Did someone accidentally drop the lit cigarette that sparked the pile of garbage by the wall and caused the house fire? Or did someone intentionally hold it to a piece of paper until the pile was ablaze?

In the United States, researchers estimate that about one-seventh of all fires are intentionally caused, and estimates are even higher in Canada and Britain. Along with those motivated by revenge and those who simply love the thrill of the flames, arsonists can be motivated by profit, such as the business owner who burns his own store and collects the insurance money. Others do it to conceal a crime, like the thief who steals a valuable painting, then burns the entire gallery behind him. In other cases, arsonists might be religious or political extremists. They use their flames to draw attention to their causes or illustrate their hatred. Like KKK members, they set fires to demand attention and intimidate, to prey upon the fears of others.

FANNING THE FLAMES OF PROTEST

Not all fire-setting protestors are arsonists or extremists. Some simply use flames as a dramatic symbol—something to draw interviews and media cameras. In 1968, for example, a group protesting a beauty pageant in the United States wanted to show the world what they thought of society's requirements for women. They threw hairspray bottles, high-heeled shoes, girdles, makeup, and bras into a trash can and set the can on fire. The protest was shown on national television and even now, decades later, women's rights activists are sometimes disparagingly called "bra-burning feminists."

Others who have set their opinions on fire include anti–Vietnam War protestors in the 1960s and '70s. As American men who were too young to legally vote or drink were conscripted to fight in Vietnam, a student protest group called the Vietnam Day Committee in Berkeley, California, organized a public ceremony where they burned the draft card of a young man who refused to become a soldier. And as other men fled to such countries as Canada or Sweden, or escaped the draft by marrying or enrolling in college, protests featuring burning draft cards continued.

People who set flags on fire are often protesting the acts of their own countries. In Canada, for example, English-speaking activists spoke out against French language laws in 1990 by burning the flag of Quebec, the province where the majority of French-speaking citizens live. In Northern Ireland, protestors have repeatedly burned the British flag, rejecting British rule of their traditional lands.

In 1984, an American youth activist named Gregory Lee Johnson marched through the streets of Dallas as part of a political protest, and set a United States flag on fire. A Texas court found him guilty of "desecrating a venerated object," fined him $2000, and sentenced him to a year in prison. Johnson appealed the decision, all the way to the Supreme Court. There, judges ruled that his act of flag burning was part of having free speech, a basic right of every American. They ruled that because his act was a political statement, not intended to hurt anyone, it was protected and legal.

Despite the court's decision, many Americans consider

flag burning a way of betraying one's own country—a type of treason. In places such as Denmark and Finland, the courts agree. In those nations, it's illegal to burn or deface flags and protestors must find other ways to express their views.

In very rare cases, people have gone far beyond burning bras, draft cards, or flags and actually set fire to themselves as a kind of protest. This form of suicide is called self-immolation. It first made international headlines in 1963, when a Vietnamese Buddhist monk named Thích Quảng Đức drove to Saigon, seated himself at the edge of a busy city intersection, doused himself with gasoline, and set himself on fire. He was protesting the persecution of Buddhists in South Vietnam, and the war in which Vietnamese people were killing each other. According to witnesses, including a *New York Times* reporter, he remained completely still until he died.

As the United States became involved in the Vietnam War

Protest or Riot?

After white police officers arrested a black man in Watts, Los Angeles, in 1965, neighborhood residents took to the streets in anger. The crowd soon turned violent, with people stuffing lit rags into alcohol- or gas-filled bottles and throwing the homemade bombs into businesses. Six hundred buildings were destroyed by the flames.

in the late 1960s, a few American citizens followed Thích Quảng Đức's lead. The first was an anti-war protestor in her 80s. The second was a 31-year-old father of four who handed his one-year-old daughter to a bystander, then set himself on fire in front of the Pentagon. Two others followed.

In 1998, a young man from Tibet, living in exile in India, set himself on fire and burned 95 percent of his body. He died in hospital the next day. Several Tibetan exiles had been enduring a hunger strike for more than a month, hoping to persuade the United Nations to become more actively involved in freeing Tibet from Chinese rule. When Indian police broke up the hunger strike, Thupten Ngodup decided extreme action was necessary, and burned himself for his cause.

The Dalai Lama, the most famous of Tibet's exiles, was torn by the event. He said that although he understood the strong feelings behind the suicide, it was still violence—the same sort of violence he was struggling to end.

For a protester, a blaze is an attention-getter far stronger than a billboard, a pamphlet, or a sign—it forces the world to stop and look. Perhaps it's that same built-in instinct to pay attention to fire that makes it such a strong symbol of love as well. Just as we recognize the danger of an open flame, we recognize the mystery of candlelight, the joy of a dark sky ablaze with lanterns, or the happiness of a wedding day fire. In love, in hate, or in protest, flame is the most extreme example of all.

SIX

Ready, Aim, Fire!

FIRE AND WAR

The Chinese goddess Nu Wa created a perfect world of peace and order, filled with gentle streams and shady trees, flower-carpeted meadows and picturesque mountainsides. Zhu Rong, the god of fire, had helped her create her masterpiece. But so had Gong Gong, the god of water. And Gong Gong was so pleased with his contributions that he spent from morning to night bragging about his role. He was vital to the world, he boasted. People could not live without him, and no force was as powerful as he was.

Zhu Rong couldn't listen any longer. He had contributed much more than Gong Gong. He was sure of it! And no force was more powerful than fire. He confronted Gong Gong and the two gods began to argue. At first, the winds trembled as they hurled words back and forth. But then, as the gods broke into outright battle, the Earth itself seemed to shake. Zhu Rong woke his boiling volcanoes and spewed out lava, while Gong Gong sent tidal waves crashing against the land.

Rising into the sky in their fury, they affected the air. In

Zhu Rong's hands, lightning bolts became fiery weapons, and Gong Gong made rain stream from the clouds. Then, just when Zhu Rong seemed to be gaining the upper hand, Gong Gong grew so furious that he rammed his head against the mountaintop that held up the sky.

Certain they were going to be killed by the lava, the waves, the lightning, and the storm, the people of Earth prayed frantically to Nu Wa. When she heard their pleas, she stared at the world in shock. Gong Gong's attack on the mountaintop had torn open the sky, and the ceiling of the world was threatening to fall. Quickly, she gathered stones and used great heat to melt them. With the bubbling fluid, she managed to patch the tear. Then she turned a giant sea turtle upside down and used its legs to prop up the sky.

Such power made Zhu Rong and Gong Gong stop in their tracks. The goddess had used the tools of their own domains to repair the damage they had caused. Humbled by her strength, they retreated to their own sectors of the sky, where they now live in tenuous peace.

Just as the battle of Zhu Rong and Gong Gong sent lightning and lava pouring onto the Earth, human wars have incorporated every conceivable type of fire. The earliest uses of fire in battle were the most obvious ones. Soldiers might burn an enemy army's storehouses, leaving them without food. They might pepper the thatched roofs of people's homes with flaming arrows, setting entire villages alight. They might even burn the forests around their own cities, so enemies couldn't hide under the cover of the trees.

In the ninth century BCE, armies in Assyria in what is now the Middle East filled clay pots with fire and hurled them at enemy soldiers. The search for ways to throw more flames and throw them farther eventually helped lead to the development of catapults. And by 360 BCE, pots filled with burning pitch were being catapulted from Greek harbors to crash on the wooden decks of enemy ships. In fact, with the arrival of the catapult, armies across the Mediterranean discovered that when faced with an enemy navy, fire was the most effective weapon of all.

Born about 290 BCE, in the city of Syracuse on the eastern coast of Sicily in the Mediterranean, Archimedes was a mathematical genius. Numbers and shapes fascinated him and he devoted every spare hour to study. Some of Archimedes' most ambitious creations came about when the Roman army invaded Syracuse and King Hieron II asked his mathematician to put his mind to work. Archimedes complied, and created massive cranes that would drop rocks on the enemy soldiers, huge claws to lift ships out of the water, and cannon-like machines to hurl rocks through the air.

Then he had an even more dramatic idea. If a small curved mirror could concentrate the sun's rays and set dried leaves on fire, what could an enormous one achieve? While some historians aren't convinced that Archimedes actually succeeded in building the mirrors, stories from that time say he used hundreds of small pieces to create a giant parabolic reflector in the Syracuse harbor. When the sun's rays hit the

Pots with Pinch

Fire wasn't the only thing thrown at opposing armies. In Constantinople, soldiers also hurled pots full of scorpions or bags of poisonous dust.

reflector, they could be concentrated and aimed at the Roman ships, setting them on fire.

Unfortunately, these weapons weren't enough to keep the Romans from ransacking the city, and they weren't enough to save Archimedes himself. He was captured in his workshop by Roman forces. When he ordered the soldiers not to touch his papers and calculations, he was killed on the spot.

GREEK FIRE

Almost a thousand years after Archimedes designed his mirror, people discovered a new type of fire even more dangerous to enemy ships and soldiers. Across Europe and the Middle East, a terrible rumor spread: the army of Constantinople was

Mirroring the Myth

For centuries, tales of Archimedes' fire-mirror were treated as myth. But in the 1700s, a French mathematician named Georges-Louis Leclerc reproduced the effect. Today, at the Odeillo-Font-Romeau Solar Furnace in France, a parabolic mirror concentrates sunlight and produces temperatures of 33,000°C (59,400°F). The heat is used to melt iron and produce steel.

using flames shot from tubes and pumps to annihilate their enemies. These flames were almost supernatural—water couldn't extinguish them.

This new weapon of Constantinople became known throughout the region as Greek fire. Although the exact formula was eventually lost, the concoction may have been a mixture of pine resin, sulfur, and petroleum. Like a stovetop grease fire in a modern kitchen, the burning pitch would have been water resistant—splashing it would have only spread the mixture and the flames. It would have been thin enough to pump through a tube, yet thick enough to keep burning as it reached the air.

According to some histories, this new type of fire was invented by a Greek-born architect named Kallinikos. For six summers, Arab troops from the south had surrounded Constantinople, cutting off trade and leaving the people trapped within the city. But when the seventh summer arrived, the city leaders adopted Kallinikos's invention. With bronze tanks and hoses mounted on the walls of the city and on the bows of their ships, they blasted the Arab forces with flame.

Although the weapon was rarely used (probably to help prevent the formula from falling into enemy hands), Greek fire saved the city again in 941 CE, when Igor the Russian attacked Constantinople with thousands of ships. He was met by 15 fireships shooting flames from their bows, sides, and sterns. Defenseless against fire that couldn't be doused with water, the foreign ships disintegrated. Sailors threw themselves into the sea, where they were burned or drowned in their heavy armor.

Despite the secrecy of Constantinople's leaders, the use of Greek fire slowly spread. In 1191, Christian armies from Europe were laying siege to the town of Acre in what is now Israel. Someone from Damascus—a man whose name has since been lost in history—secretly contacted the leaders of the city and promised that he could set fire to the opposing army if he was allowed within the walls. After negotiations, he was smuggled inside.

Boiling petroleum and other ingredients in huge copper pots, the young man created roiling balls of fire. But at first, he left them unused.

The Christians had built huge wooden towers, planning to roll them up to the walls of the city and climb over the defenses. The man from Damascus filled small pots with a secret mixture and threw them at the towers. Soldiers on both sides held their breath. But nothing happened. The potions inside the pots seemed powerless. Filled with new confidence, the Christian soldiers rushed up the stairways inside the towers. But just as they were pressed together in masses, waiting to storm the walls, the man from Damascus unleashed his roiling balls of fire. As they struck the towers, already soaked with the unknown, "unsuccessful" potions,

Gassy Guesses

If Greek fire was a petroleum-based product, then the unsuccessful potions used by the man from Damascus may have been a type of gasoline. Once he soaked the wooden towers, they would have burned quickly and fiercely.

the wood burst into flames, burning so quickly that the soldiers couldn't escape.

POWERFUL POWDER

In parts of ancient China, a chemical called saltpeter appeared naturally on the surface of the earth, a fine white crust left where plants or animal waste had decomposed. For years, women had occasionally added it as a spice for stews and meats, throwing a little in the pot when they were short of salt. So maybe it was a wife of an alchemist who happened to throw some saltpeter in the soup and spilled a bit into the fire itself. Pop! Pop! Pop! Although harmless, the noise and the burst of light when chemical met flame made alchemists think saltpeter might have great powers.

Eventually, these ancient alchemists—men searching for the secret of eternal life—discovered that by scraping charred pieces of wood into fine black dust, then adding saltpeter and sulfur, they could create small explosions. Today, scientists know that sulfur ignites easily, and charcoal burns at high temperatures. Their combined heat would release the oxygen stored in saltpeter with a sudden burst of energy. But the alchemists saw it differently. Sulfur, they said, was a positive material, like the light of the sun. Saltpeter was negative, like the light of the moon. When the two met, an explosion was bound to occur.

Whatever the reason for the explosion, the alchemists called their creation "fire chemical" or "fire drug"—which we now know as gunpowder. The powder, with its ear-splitting bangs and showers of lights, was soon being used in firecrackers and fireworks to entertain nobles and emperors. But it wasn't long before some of these displays gave the aristocrats new ideas for war.

In the 11th century, the Sung dynasty in China was a highly developed and successful society. The capital city was larger than Rome at the time. Despite advanced technology that included compasses and printing presses, the kingdom was constantly being threatened by barbarian invaders from central Asia.

In 1044, Emperor Jen Tsung was offered two formulas for new weapons that could be used in battle. Both included gunpowder. With the first, soldiers could hurl small bombs at their enemies that would burst into flames. With the second, they could send smoke pouring onto the field.

For a few years, the noise and smoke caused by these devices kept the barbarians at bay, but they wouldn't stay frightened forever. By 1083, soldiers were developing a new weapon—a lump of gunpowder wrapped in paper and glued to the shaft of an arrow with pine resin. An archer could light a fuse just before firing, and send a burning arrow streaking toward his enemies. Soon after that, metal balls were equipped with hooks and filled with gunpowder, to be fired by catapults and cling to wooden walls and towers, where they would explode.

These early gunpowder weapons still caused more light and sound than actual fire. But seeing the potential in his new formulas, Emperor Jen took control of sulfur and saltpeter production. Obviously, these chemicals were too dangerous for ordinary people to make and use. He managed to keep their production secret until 1127, when invaders finally captured the capital city and the Chi dynasty began.

Under the Chi emperors, scientists learned to produce saltpeter artificially, so it no longer had to be painstakingly collected from the earth. Then they learned that if they added more saltpeter to their charcoal and sulfur formula, the powder would create a larger explosion with more flame.

Soon, gunpowder-filled weapons known as Heaven-Shaking Thunder Crash Bombs were scorching battlefields and echoing across the hills to be heard up to 50 kilometers (30 miles) away. When soldiers filled the bombs with sharp pieces of metal and pottery, they discovered that the shrapnel from the explosions could pierce the iron armor of their enemies.

THE FIRST FIREARMS

In 1233, Chinese soldiers began using fire lances—long tubes of thick paper, filled with flammable materials and gunpowder. Each soldier carried a small pot of fire with him. He would kindle his fire lance, and flames would shoot more than a body-length in front of him. By 1259, these paper tubes had been replaced by lengths of bamboo. And instead of filling them with flammable things, soldiers began filling them with small pellets that peppered enemies when the tubes were lit.

Despite these innovations, the Mongols still managed to overwhelm the Chi forces and conquer China in 1274. Determined to take over the production of these fascinating new weapons, they fired the Chi scientists and put their own researchers into the gunpowder laboratories. Unfortunately, they didn't realize just how dangerous saltpeter could be and in 1280, the entire arsenal exploded, killing the researchers.

With new scientists in place, the Mongols eventually conquered the mysteries of gunpowder and made their own innovations. They created larger-scale tubes to fire bigger objects over longer distances: the first cannons. Then they turned their attention to the bamboo tubes, and replaced them with iron. By 1325, soldiers were loading their long iron tubes with gunpowder, inserting heated wires in the bases, and firing the world's first guns.

By this time, the formula for gunpowder was being traded to the Arab world and spreading quickly throughout Europe. In the late 1330s, cities from London to Florence were mounting small cannons to help defend their walls. And in 1346, the combination of longbows and gunfire that roared across the battlefield like thunder allowed English King Edward III and his 12,000 men to wipe out 30,000 to 40,000 French soldiers. Some historians estimate that a third of all French nobles were killed in the Battle of Crécy. And others

Cannon Fodder

In 1453, Arab leader Mehmed hired a metalworker named Urban to create the largest gun ever built. It took 50 teams of oxen to move the massive cannon and 700 men to supply the gunpowder and load the barrel. Mehmed used his new weapon to lay siege to Constantinople. Two weeks later, the massive stone walls that had protected the city for ten centuries had been torn apart. The stone fortifications that surrounded almost every city in Europe were suddenly obsolete.

point to the English victory, and the use of longbows and guns, as the end of the age of knights and chivalry.

Obviously, the discovery of gunpowder made all previous weapons—from arrows to catapults to Greek fire—seem like toys. With the explosive power of fire locked within iron barrels, soldiers could kill from greater distances and with greater speed than ever before. The secrets of gunpowder and guns were traded from one society to another, across the continents and eventually across the oceans, creating the greatest changes in warfare until the 20th century.

THINGS THAT GO BOOM

In the 1860s, while other scientists were still exploring the possibilities of gunpowder, a Swedish chemist named Alfred Nobel chose a different path. Along with his father and his brother, he was working to perfect an explosive made out of an oily liquid called nitroglycerin.

Previous explosives such as gunpowder worked because of something called deflagration. As each layer of the material burned, it heated and ignited the next layer. Nitroglycerin, however, worked because of something new—detonation. In detonation, a shock wave of energy compressed the material until it was under so much pressure that it ignited. Nobel used gunpowder to create an initial shock wave that turned some of his nitroglycerin into gas—gas that took up thousands of times more room than the initial oil did. The pressure of this gas to escape raised the temperature within the nitroglycerin so high that the entire stick would ignite and explode.

This sort of detonation was less predictable but more powerful than deflagration. If handled with extreme care and set alight in precisely the right way, nitroglycerin could be 10 times stronger than gunpowder, allowing engineers to blast tunnels out of solid stone, or soldiers to lay perilous landmines.

Unfortunately, just as Nobel was meeting with a prominent businessman to request new funding, his younger brother was attempting to simplify the method used to produce nitroglycerin. In an explosion that shook nearby buildings, shattered windows, and obliterated the family's laboratory, the brother and four coworkers were instantly killed. Nobel's father suffered a stroke a month later.

Despite the tragedy—and against the wishes of the city of Stockholm, where the explosion had taken place—Nobel opened a new laboratory on a barge moored conveniently just outside city limits. And orders poured in from around the world. To railroad builders in the United States, miners in Australia, and weapons factories in Europe, this new tool was too powerful to be ignored.

Nobel had failed to realize one important fact. His invention became less stable and more dangerous as it aged. The year after his business started to grow, tragedies involving nitroglycerin began occurring around the world. Ships sank and warehouses where it had been stored suddenly blew up. In San Francisco, a leaking crate of nitroglycerin was delivered to the docks and promptly detonated, killing 10 people and turning an entire block of the city into rubble. Nobel's own factories—there were two by this time—exploded.

Hated around the world, but more stubbornly attached to his idea than ever, Nobel set up his own private laboratory and began a quest to make nitroglycerin stable. With his own life at risk, he mixed the oil into a range of materials, from sawdust to charcoal, trying to create a solid explosive.

According to legend, it was pure chance that Nobel happened to be standing nearby when a worker dropped a box of the oil onto a bed of clay. Noticing how the clay absorbed it, he immediately set about creating an explosive stick of mixed clay and nitroglycerin. He named it dynamite, based on the Greek word for strength.

His new product was five times stronger than gunpowder, safe to store, and easy to use in tunnels and tight spaces. By 1874, his factories were producing more than several thousand tonnes each year, and Nobel was shockingly rich.

Railroad builders and miners found the most obvious uses for dynamite. But war strategists were quick to follow. In 1870, Napoleon III invaded Prussia and discovered that the Prussian army had devised its own ways to apply the new explosive. After his forts were blown up and his bridges destroyed, Napoleon and his soldiers were surrounded and taken prisoner about six weeks after his first declaration of war.

In the 1890s, as Nobel grew older and his health deteriorated, he began to reflect on the deaths caused by dynamite: both the accidental deaths in factory explosions and industrial accidents, and the wartime deaths caused by dynamite-inspired bombs. Determined to leave something good to counteract the bad effects his inventions had caused, he

An Active Mind

Alfred Nobel's ideas weren't limited to explosives. During his lifetime he patented plans for photography tools, blood transfusion equipment, artificial rubber, and artificial silk.

gathered four Swedish men in Paris and had them witness a will, which he then left locked in a Stockholm bank vault.

A year later, Nobel died. Those who opened his vault found the following words:

> "The whole of my remaining realizable estate shall be dealt with in the following way: The capital shall be invested . . . the interest on which shall be annually distributed in the form of prizes to those who, during the preceding year, shall have conferred the greatest benefit on mankind."

The money, he wrote, was to be divided into five portions each year. Each portion would go to someone who had made a great impact on a specific field: physics, chemistry, medicine, literature, and peace.

From the profits of dynamite, Nobel had left money to form the base of the world's most respected awards—the Nobel Prizes.

FIRE FROM THE SKY

Chinese armies were hurling fire bombs at enemy walls in the 14th century and Alfred Nobel invented dynamite in 1867. It's no surprise, then, that nations were dropping fire bombs from the air by the early 20th century. Filled with a small amount of explosives and a large amount of highly combustible fuel—often magnesium, phosphorus, or petroleum jelly—these bombs could incinerate neighborhoods of wooden buildings, and even burn through steel.

In World War II, fire bombs were used by both German and Allied forces. And in London, so many bombs fell for so many days that the period between September 7, 1940, and

May 16, 1941, became known as the Blitz. Short for *blitz-krieg,* or lightning war, the Blitz began when a few misdirected German planes dropped bombs on London, and Britain retaliated by bombing the German city of Berlin. Outraged, Hitler ordered his air force to bomb civilian and military targets in London around the clock. He was determined to get revenge for the British attacks, destroy his enemy's morale, and force Britain to surrender. German squadrons swooped over the city, dropping fire bombs on residential neighborhoods and killing hundreds of people as they scrambled for shelter.

As Britain struggled to organize better radar stations, anti-aircraft guns, and air raid warning systems, the bombs continued to fall. Sometimes, planes would drop their fire bombs at the same time as delayed-explosive bombs, making work extremely dangerous for the city's firefighters. They were called to house fires, business fires, block fires, and church fires, knowing that at any moment, they could literally be blown to pieces.

As the months passed, the bombing intensified. In December, German planes dropped 600 tonnes (660 tons) of

Ferocious Fire

On March 10, 1945, American planes dropped fire bombs on the wooden neighborhoods of Tokyo, turning 41 square kilometers (16 square miles) into charred ruins. Between 80,000 and 100,000 people died.

bombs and 4000 canisters of highly flammable chemicals. On December 8, 115,000 fire bombs sparked more than 1500 fires in the city. And on December·29, 22,000 fire bombs, starting blazes that reached 980°C (1800°F), killed more than 3700 people and injured 5000 more.

To spread fear and disable Britain's trading abilities, the bombers began targeting port cities and harbors around London. But on May 10, they returned to the capital one last time, starting 2000 fires that damaged parts of the royal family's palace, the Houses of Parliament, the Tower of London, and 5000 homes.

Eventually, as Britain's defenses improved and the Allies began to put pressure on Germany, the Blitz abated. But signs of the fire bombs, from burned-out shells of buildings to city blocks filled with rubble, could still be seen throughout London decades after the end of the war.

The fire bombs of World War II—the ones the Germans dropped on British targets, the ones the Americans dropped on Tokyo, and the ones the Allies dropped on the historic sites of Germany—probably destroyed more property and killed more civilians than any other previous weapon. And yet, as the war ended, countries made no move to destroy or ban their flame-filled weapons. Instead, they concentrated on new and improved fire bombing technology.

A NEW GREEK FIRE

On June 8, 1972, a South Vietnamese aircraft winged over jungles and small villages. In its belly, it carried an incendiary bomb—a bomb filled with flammable gel called napalm, meant to coat and burn everything it touched.

The bomb was intended for the fortifications of the North Vietnamese army a short distance away. But as the plane arced over the small South Vietnamese village of Trang Bang, something went wrong and the weapon dropped too early. Within seconds, the village was smothered in flames. Screaming, people raced down the streets toward open air, their clothes burning off their bodies.

A photographer named Nick Ut was in the village that day, and snapped an image of nine-year-old Kim Phuc Phan Thi fleeing naked from the flames. The picture was printed around the world, shocking sheltered North Americans as they scanned their daily newspapers.

Developed by the United States during World War II, napalm was the name for a chemical powder made of naphthalene and palmitate. Mixed together and added to gasoline, these chemicals formed a highly flammable gel that

Survival Story

Photographer Nick Ut won a Pulitzer Prize for his photograph of the napalm attack. Against all expectations, Kim Phuc Phan Thi survived the bombing. She returned to her village after 14 months in a Saigon hospital. As an adult, she moved to Canada, became a peace activist, and founded an organization to help child victims of war.

could be dropped in bombs. Specially designed ignition devices caused the gel to explode upon impact.

Napalm was first used on a Nazi fuel depot in France on July 17, 1944. In later years, it was used by Greece, Mexico, and even United Nations forces. But its use in the Vietnam War, including the accidental attack on the village of Trang Bang, made napalm famous (and hated) around the world.

In 1980, the United Nations passed an agreement to ban the use of napalm on civilian targets. Although it didn't sign the agreement, the United States eventually destroyed its stores of napalm in 2001.

THE FIRES OF REVENGE

In 1988, deep in debt after a long war with Iran, the leader of Iraq began looking for a way to recover the billions of dollars his weapons and soldiers had cost. What Saddam Hussein saw, looking past his country's border, was the tiny nation of Kuwait—where vast oil stores lay below the sands of the desert.

In 1990, Iraq accused Kuwait of exporting more oil than it was allowed to under international law. Then it charged Kuwait with sucking oil from an underground field on the border between the nations, essentially stealing Iraq's supply. When negotiations failed, Hussein sent 150,000 soldiers over the border, straight toward the capital city. Kuwait's small, 20,000-person army was hopelessly overwhelmed, and the fighting was mainly over within 24 hours.

What Hussein had failed to predict was the response of the United States. Furious that one of its major oil suppliers had been so casually conquered, the U.S. sent 400,000 soldiers to the border of Saudi Arabia and Kuwait. They were joined by 200,000 more from other United Nations countries. On January 17, 1991, after several demands to withdraw had been met with silence from Hussein, the combined UN forces attacked from the air. For more than a month, bombers swept over both Kuwait and Iraq—100,000 flights. On February 24, the soldiers moved in to surround the capital and take back control of Kuwait.

Many Iraqi soldiers surrendered or deserted and escaped into the desert. But Hussein's most elite units began an orderly retreat back through the desert toward the Iraq border. And along the way, they began one of the most devastating actions of the war. They set more than 700 oil wells on fire, vandalizing the emergency shut-off measures and destroying safety equipment. Soon, 6 million barrels of oil a day were being transformed into a blanket of black smoke that cloaked the entire region in poison. In the desert, seas of oil rippled over the sand, only to be lit by random sparks and turn into unstoppable flames. From the air, the country looked like a giant black cloud punctuated by roaring jets of fire. The flames were visible even from space.

With a shortage of roads into the desert, a shortage of water, and the safety equipment destroyed, it took eight months to extinguish the wells. Explosives experts combed the areas around the wells for land mines, drivers took heavy equipment fitted with heat shields far into the desert, and workers dug three massive lagoons to hold seawater, which was then piped into the desert via an oil pipeline.

Just as the victims of napalm were often villagers caught in the wrong place, the victims of the oil well fires were the citizens of the Middle East who lived through months of choking smoke, the journalists or workers caught in blazing oil lakes or suddenly sparked flames, and the firefighters who battled in a foreign country in unimaginable heat and in constant danger. They personally bore witness to the devastation caused by the use of fire in war.

SEVEN

A Fiery Planet

FIRE AND NATURE

In her dreams, the fire goddess Pele heard the relentless beat of a drum. On and on it went, echoing across the Hawaiian Islands and sparking Pele's curiosity. She left her home, the bubbling crater of the volcano Kilauea, and began searching for the source of the sound.

Finally, she found it. Performing for a crowd of his people, Prince Lohiau was drumming, singing, and dancing. Pele was so intrigued by the handsome prince that she turned into a beautiful woman and joined the festivities. Before long, Lohiau was enthralled.

"Where did you come from?" he asked.

"From the direction of the rising sun."

"Until now," said Lohiau, "I thought there were beautiful women in my kingdom."

Pele had surpassed all his expectations. After looking at her, every other woman seemed dull and lifeless. Without knowing that she was a goddess, Lohiau asked her to marry him.

For several days, they enjoyed their status as newlyweds. But soon, Pele grew bored.

"I must return to my island," she told him. "Stay faithful while I am gone."

When she left, the strong young prince was heartbroken, and soon died of grief. Pele's heart had also been affected. Missing her husband, she sent her favorite sister Hiiaka' to retrieve him. Hiiaka' found the prince's body, brought it back to life, and nursed him to health before traveling with him to Pele's volcano.

But Pele's temper was just as hot as her volcanic home. Her sister had been gone so long that Pele was sure Hiiaka' must have fallen in love with the prince. In rage, she destroyed her sister's seaside home.

When Hiiaka' and Lohiau finally reached the volcano, they tried to explain their delay. Pele was too furious to listen. She opened a river of lava between the two and ordered her other sisters to kill Lohiau. Obediently, they transformed his body into stone.

BURNING AND BUBBLING ROCK

To the ancient people of the Hawaiian Islands, the fiery temper of a volcano was one of Earth's most powerful forces. Now, hundreds of years after storytellers wove tales of Pele, modern scientists know that the inside of our planet really is a realm of fire, just as uncontrollable and just as dangerous as it was generations ago.

More than 5000 kilometers (3000 miles) below us, the Earth's center is a dense iron core. Between this galactic-sized stone and the thin solid crust that supports us are layers of fiery liquid rock: the outer core of molten iron and nickel, and the mantle, 2900 kilometers (1800 miles) deep. The planet's surface is composed of enormous continental plates that "float" on the mantle's sea of molten rock, or magma. In a way, the plates act like the hard chocolate coating on a dipped ice cream cone. Imagine you've bitten into the chocolate just once, and the coating has cracked into large chunks. Those chunks are just like the plates that cover the Earth. And their edges never seem to meet quite perfectly. There are always a few places where the ice cream—or the burning magma—seeps through.

Along the borders of the continental plates, where the plates are jostling against one another, the pressure of the magma beneath sometimes builds until it forces its way up to the Earth's surface in the form of a volcano. Like the volcano goddess Pele, magma can be enormously destructive, burning everything in its wake. The liquid rock ranges from 800°C to 1200°C (1470°F to 2200°F). And just as Pele created new stone out of her husband, the volcanoes spew forth lava that hardens into new rock on the Earth's surface.

Lava is a bubbling mixture of melted rock and gas. Explosive and red hot, it can burst from a mountaintop and leave behind a trail of destruction. All over the Earth, wherever continental plates meet, it's trying to force its way to the surface. Sometimes it succeeds. Under the oceans, it boils up to meet the seawater and chills into high ridges or sculptural globules. Under land, it presses up and up until the crust itself changes and a volcano is born.

For years, these volcanoes can slowly rise into the sky. In the shapes of wide, low domes, steep concave curves, or looming cones, they swell under the pressure from the liquid rock beneath them. And when the pressure finally reaches a critical point—too great for the crust to withstand—lava explodes forth. The ground tears open and smoke and molten rock spew into the air, often with earth-shaking violence: a volcanic eruption.

One of the largest eruptions in modern history occurred

on the mainly uninhabited island of Krakatoa near Java, Indonesia. In 1883, the nearest city on Java—Batavia—was a bustling trading port. European colonists lived in ornate mansions along the wide streets of the upper town, while vendors on the frenzied lower streets hawked fruit, vegetables, crafts, pets, and tropical birds. The city boasted telephone service, a public tram, gas streetlights, and even an ice factory. In the surrounding countryside, plantation owners worked huge swaths of land, while prospectors scoured the hillsides.

Just after midnight on May 10, the lighthouse keeper at First Point on Java made a note in his logbook: earthquake. On May 15, a larger tremor shook the island. Five days after that, one of the town leaders in nearby Sumatra sent a worried telegram—earthquakes were almost constantly shaking the coast of the island.

He was right to worry. That same morning, a white plume rose from one of the four summits on Krakatoa, funneled far up into the sky, then spread like a blanket until it almost entirely blocked the sun. Ash began to rain on the islands.

To the residents of Java, it seemed as if the air itself was vibrating. And while the earthquakes common to the area always stopped after a few seconds or minutes, this vibration continued. When two government officials set off by boat to see what was actually happening, they found the beach around Krakatoa transformed into a cauldron of fire, ripped open by the tremors.

The peak continued to smoke and occasionally tremor, but it seemed as if the worst was over. People went back to their usual activities for a few months. Until, on August 27, the entire island of Krakatoa exploded. First came sounds like distant cannon fire, growing steadily louder. Then huge bubbles of smoke rose from the peaks. And the ocean seemed to slosh back and forth, as if it were water in a bucket carried by a running child. By the afternoon, thick smoke had blotted out the sun and Batavia was in complete darkness, broken only by the showers of fire erupting from the mountaintop. Ash rained down and huge waves sent people scurrying for high ground. Soon, chunks of hot rock were falling from the sky, smashing into homes and the decks of ships.

By the evening, flaming ash was falling on the surrounding islands and the waves were 10 stories high. When at last the explosions culminated in a jet of fire and ash that flew 38 kilometers (24 miles) into the air, residents of the seaside towns on the surrounding islands—their eardrums shattered by the noise—were already racing inland. Tsunamis swept the region, tearing buildings from their foundations and washing away entire villages.

On tiny Sebesi Island to the northeast, tidal waves swept about 3000 people into the ocean, tore trees and plants from their roots, and left the land looking as if no one had ever lived there. Families were separated in the rush to escape. Many people's homes were demolished—others disappeared completely. More than 40 kilometers (25 miles)

Moving Mountains

As the continental plates continue to press against one another, the volcanic peak of Krakatoa is slowly rebuilding itself. It's now visible once more from the shores of Java.

away on southern Sumatra, people were hit by waves that still carried blistering hot lava flows. Their burned bodies were found floating in debris. In total, more than 36,000 people died.

When the eruptions were over, the 790-meter (2600-foot) summit of Krakatoa had entirely disappeared. Like a shipwreck, it sank beneath the ocean and left behind only debris.

In Indonesia, it was the tsunamis caused by the volcano that proved most devastating. But other volcanoes kill with fire directly. In the year 79 CE, the ground near Mount Vesuvius in what is now Italy began to shake. Then the mountain sent a stream of smoke into the air, and hot stone crashed through the roofs of homes in the surrounding cities of Pompeii, Herculaneum, and Stabiae. Soon, lava surged down the mountain, completely burying Herculaneum beneath more than six stories of boiling rock. The burning rivers continued along their paths, demolishing Pompeii and Stabiae and leaving nothing but ash and rock in their wakes. Almost 1600 years later, the mountain erupted again, killing 4000 people who lived near its base.

And volcanoes are just as active today. On May 18, 1980, Mount St. Helens in the northwestern United States erupted, sending a 250°C (480°F) cloud of burning gas and debris— hot enough to broil meat or melt tin—shooting into the air. The imposing peak of the mountain was suddenly a charred crater, and lava flowed down the slopes. As the rivers of molten rock writhed through the valleys, they set everything in their paths on fire. Fifty-seven people were killed, along with thousands of animals. Bridges, railway tracks, and 300 kilometers (185 miles) of the nearby highway were destroyed.

GREAT BALL OF FIRE

The oceans of magma beneath the Earth's crust are so massive they are difficult for us to imagine. Yet the fiery globe that rises in our sky each morning is infinitely larger—a million Earths would fit inside it. Even though the sun is 150 million kilometers (93 million miles) away, this ball of burning, glowing gas is so powerful that it provides the energy necessary for life on Earth. It creates our days and nights, its light provides the energy necessary for plants to grow, and its heat causes the winds that bring our weather.

If the sun were a normal fire like the ones we sit around at campsites, it would have burned up its supply of fuel millions of years ago. Yet scientists estimate that it has been steadily burning for 4.6 billion years. The secret lies in the heat and pressure in the sun's core—pressure so intense that it forces atoms to collide and break, releasing more energy in a second than all the humans on Earth have used in 100,000 years.

From the center, where temperatures reach 2.2 million degrees Celsius (4 million degrees Fahrenheit), searing hot gases rise toward the sun's surface, then circle back down, like heat waves in a giant oven. But the heat of the sun isn't entirely constant, and even minor changes can have surprisingly large effects on Earth.

Powerful Puffs

Scientists estimate that the amount of energy released in the explosion of Mount St. Helens in 1980 equaled 27,000 atomic bombs.

In 1610, an Italian scientist named Galileo found a way to look at the sun through a telescope without damaging his eyes. He pointed the lens at the sun, but projected the magnified image onto a screen, which he could then safely study. What he discovered was that the surface of the sun was always changing, with dark patches called sunspots appearing, moving, and disappearing. When he released his findings, other scientists began watching and counting these spots and found that the number rose and fell in a fairly predictable cycle.

Then, in the mid-1600s, the number of sunspots dramatically decreased. At the same time, the Earth grew colder. Rivers that were usually ice-free all year suddenly froze solid and snow remained on the ground in summer. Scientists now call this period the Little Ice Age and many believe that decreases in the sun's activity could have caused Earth's more extensive ice ages as well.

The largest sunspots are bigger than the Earth itself and, as the number of spots increases, so does the number of solar flares. A solar flare is a kind of massive explosion caused by unstable magnetism on the sun's surface. With the power of a billion megatons of dynamite, they send burning gas and plasma shooting into space. The effects of this sort of discharge reach Earth in minutes, as the radiation hits the atmosphere. Radio waves are skewed, satellites slow down, and oxygen transforms into ozone.

One to two days after a solar flare, another kind of effect can be felt. If the flare is on the side of the sun nearest Earth, it can send a solar wind rocketing through space toward the planet's atmosphere and magnetic field. As the wind hits and buffets the Earth—something scientists call a geomagnetic storm—the northern lights spread over the sky and radiation levels in the atmosphere rise. Sometimes they rise so high that researchers suggest planes fly at lower altitudes. In 1989, as a particularly violent wind rocketed toward Earth, astronauts on the Mir space station absorbed as much radiation in a few hours as they would have in a year on the ground.

As scientists continue to study sunspots, solar flares, and geomagnetic storms, some are beginning to believe that these events affect even more minute aspects of daily life on Earth, from temperatures and wind speeds to the abilities of animals. Dolphins and whales, for example, may not be able to navigate as well during these disruptions of the atmosphere. Many biologists believe marine mammals, migratory birds, and maybe even humans have a unique kind of internal compass—a small amount of a mineral called magnetite, wrapped in nerve cells. When solar flares change the Earth's geomagnetic field, it's more difficult for animals to find their paths. In fact, so many homing pigeon races have gone awry during geomagnetic storms that organizers now check for solar flare activity before beginning their events.

Without doubt, the sun is the most powerful fire in our lives. Yet we probably understand its methods and effects

Sun Struck

The way Galileo used a screen to look at the sun was a kind of camera obscura. Very basic forms of these are called pinhole cameras, and can easily be made at home with a cardboard box, a roll of film, aluminum foil, and black paper.

less than we understand the workings of our campfires. As scientists do more research, they realize the sun gives us much more than warmth and suntans. When we get caught in a sudden storm, hear only static on our favorite radio station, or find ourselves "turned around" and lost just a few blocks from home, it's possible we should look to the sky for answers.

STATIC ELECTRICITY ON A PLANETARY SCALE

While magma roils beneath the Earth's surface and the sun seethes far above the atmosphere, another fiery force of nature attacks from the space between. Every second, lightning strikes the Earth about 100 times, sparking fires in South American rainforests, Alaskan tundra, and African brush. Each of these bolts releases roughly 1000 volts of electricity—enough to keep a 100-watt lightbulb burning for three months.

This type of fire is all about static. Everything on Earth is made of atoms and every microscopic atom is made of a nucleus, surrounded by moving electrons—like a miniature solar system. Sometimes, atoms at the bottoms of storm clouds rub against one another so much that they lose some of their electrons. They have what scientists call a negative charge. At the same time, buildings or trees on the ground might gain a few electrons, giving them a positive charge.

Opposites attract, so negative charges go in search of positives. In a lightning storm, negatively charged clouds send invisible strings of electricity down like "feelers" toward the ground. When they get close to the positive charges—zap! The negative and positive meet, creating a channel of electrical fire that surges back and forth between ground and sky. Around the current, the air grows five times hotter than the surface of the sun. And the air vibrations caused by all that "lightning-fast" heat roll out as thunder.

There are several different kinds of lightning. The most common type is an electric flash within a single cloud or between two clouds. But the type people are most likely to recognize is cloud-to-ground or fork lightning—the spectacular bolts that appear to sear down from the sky.

As scientists began to investigate lightning in the mid-1700s, American intellectual Benjamin Franklin came up with an experiment to prove that the forked flashes were created by electricity. He knew that electricity traveled through metal, so if he could prove that lightning traveled through a piece of metal, he could prove that lightning and electricity were the same thing. He suggested flying a kite in the middle of a thunderstorm. As the rain soaked the kite string, it would conduct electricity. And if a small metal object, such as a key, were attached to the bottom of the string, the current should be carried down toward the metal and through it.

Even though he'd been knocked unconscious a few times doing other experiments with electricity, Franklin rushed into a lightning storm and sent his kite spiraling high in the air. When lightning struck it, he touched his knuckle to the key. Zap! Electricity definitely traveled from the key to his body; happily, it wasn't enough to knock him out.

Franklin published his ideas in a book, and researchers in France tried the experiments as well. After they were proven successful, other scientists wanted to try it. But they weren't all as lucky.

Russian professor Georg Richmann had read Franklin's book and prepared his kite to wait for the next storm. While in a meeting one day, he heard thunder in the distance, and raced home to conduct his experiment, taking one of his colleagues along for the show. But as the kite rose into the sky, a flaming globe appeared in the air and seared toward Richmann's head. Within a heartbeat, the esteemed scientist was dead. His shoes and clothes were singed. His shocked colleague examined his body and could only find a small red spot showing the entrance point of the electricity that killed him.

The type of fiery sphere that was fatal to Richmann is called ball lightning, and is a kind of electrical fire that scientists don't yet understand. These balls are extremely rare, but they appear most often during thunderstorms. They sometimes sweep over the ground and sometimes hover in the air, either moving randomly or seemingly drawn to a

Shocking Habits

Have you ever heard the saying, "lightning never strikes the same place twice"? It's not true. For reasons that scientists can't explain, people who have been struck once are more likely to be struck again. And the Empire State Building in New York is struck by lightning about 100 times each year. Fortunately, it's protected by metal rods that channel the electricity safely to the ground.

building or object. For hundreds of years, sailors, farmers, and foresters have reported seeing these burning balls, but scientists can't accurately replicate them in the laboratory. And when people see ball lightning, they're usually too busy running to bother taking photographs.

One of the earliest reports of ball lightning dates from 1638 in Widecombe-in-the-Moor, England. A crowd was gathered inside the local church for the Sunday sermon as a violent storm thundered outside. Suddenly, a globe of flame burst through one of the windows, tore open the roof, then rebounded like a rubber ball back toward the congregation. Four people were killed, hurled into the air by some sort of explosive blast. Another 60 were burned or injured. According to a teacher who witnessed the event, some people were badly blistered while their clothes remained untouched, and some people's clothes were burned while they escaped unharmed. One man's purse appeared whole, but the coins inside had melted. Although members of the congregation

Electric Attraction

According to NASA researchers, men are four times more likely than women to be struck by lightning. Does electricity like men best? Probably not. It's possible that men just happen to be outside more often during thunderstorms, whether working or swinging metal golf clubs.

eventually realized they had been struck by some kind of lightning, many of them first thought they were facing the end of the world.

FOREST INFERNOS

In cities, where fire departments stand ready, fire damage from lightning strikes remains relatively minor. But in the wilderness, lightning can be devastating. It often strikes far from trails and access roads, making it difficult for firefighters to contain the resulting flames. Each year, it's responsible for about 10,000 forest fires in the United States and 5000 in Canada.

Some summers, soaring temperatures and low rainfall levels combine to create the perfect conditions for lightning-related forest fires. In Idaho, Montana, and Wyoming, the summer of 1998 was one of the hottest on record. When thunderstorms struck in June and July, lightning sparked fires in forests and parkland throughout the states. By late July, more than 600 soldiers were battling the Clover Mist blaze east of Yellowstone National Park. The fire had already burned 63,000 hectares (156,500 acres). Just over the Montana border, a team of Alaskan firefighters flew in to help fight the Storm Creek fire. Another blaze loomed at Warm Springs, and 500 Idaho-based firefighters fought the Eagle Bar fire in Hells Canyon.

In Yellowstone National Park, the first lightning strikes ignited small patches of woodland on May 24. By mid-July, 12 separate fires had ravaged 3400 hectares (8500 acres). Within two weeks, they had grown to envelop 40,000 hectares (99,000 acres). Much of the park was covered in stands of old-growth Douglas fir, home to towering trees that weighed up to 7700 kilograms (17,000 pounds) each. With dense carpets of dry needles surrounding each trunk, the firs acted as enormous stores of kindling and firewood.

Usually, park officials would have allowed the fires to burn unchecked. Since the early 1970s, the park service had considered forest fires to be a natural part of the forest's life cycle. Even though lightning sparked about 20 fires each summer, most of the blazes were minor and helped to clear old forest growth, creating room for new species. Between 1972 and 1987, 235 fires were allowed to burn freely. All but 15 remained small, and all were extinguished by rain or snow.

In 1998, however, the fires were far from small. As they consumed huge swaths of trees and encroached on historic park buildings, the park service enlisted help. They called in 25,000 firefighters and 4000 soldiers. Helicopters and jets dumped load after load of water and fire retardant on the forests. The effort cost $3 million per day. And it was mainly unsuccessful. The fires had grown so big that they were

Smoke Screens

Smoke from the Yellowstone National Park fires appeared as a haze in the skies above Seattle, Chicago, and Toronto, thousands of kilometers away. Scientists estimated that breathing the air in Yellowstone was like smoking four packs of cigarettes each day.

impossible to control. By the end of the summer, the park service had spent $120 million on fire fighting with barely any results. On September 11, when the blazes finally died down, it wasn't because of any human action—it was because the first autumn snowfall settled over the mountains.

THE GREAT BLACK DRAGON FIRE

Of course, lightning isn't responsible for all the world's forest fires. Many are caused by human carelessness. One of the worst blazes in recent history was sparked by a worker in the Great Black Dragon Forest of China in 1987.

The Black Dragon River runs along the border between China and what was, in 1987, the Soviet Union. Along the river an evergreen forest stretched for 800 kilometers (500 miles), and 480 kilometers (300 miles) across—larger and more intact than any in the world. The wilderness on the

Camping, Anyone?

When fighting forest fires, workers carry heat-resistant tents in their packs. Made of aluminum and fiberglass and looking like space-age foil domes, these tents are designed as emergency shelters. They can reflect 95 percent of a fire's heat and trap breathable oxygen inside.

Chinese side of the border made up a third of all the timber in the country.

In May, fire burned through the massive forest as if the trees had been strands of straw. The blaze was sparked by a newly hired, 18-year-old brush cutter named Wang Yufeng who was working at the edges of the forest, clearing a piece of land where planters would soon place new saplings. When the young man stopped to refuel his machine, he spilled a little gasoline over the metal and onto the brush below. Then, when he pulled the starter cord, a spark ignited the gas. Within moments, the dry forest floor was alight. Working frantically with shirts and blankets, the crew tried to smother the flames. But it was no use—the fire seemed to race away from them in every direction.

Fire wardens and foresters in the region had known about the high fire risk that season. Small "forest farms" in the area had been logging a lot of timber for several years in a row, and had let debris build up to waist height in some places. There had been no spring snowfall to keep the earth and vegetation damp, and spring often brought high winds that would fan any small flames. The wardens warned local landowners, sent extra rangers on patrol, and prepared firefighting helicopters.

On May 6, their fears were realized. Almost at the same time as Wang Yufeng started the brush fire in the clearing, two other blazes sparked in other areas of the forest. By May 9, the fires were expanding at 24 kilometers (15 miles) an hour. Two of them were already more than 160 kilometers (100 miles) wide. And 15 days earlier, unknown to wardens on the Chinese side of the border, several fires had also started in the Soviet-controlled part of the forest.

As the fires grew, Commander Yan Jinchun received orders to take his crew of firefighters to the outskirts of

Xilinji, a small city at the border of the forest. There, at the city's edge, lay a half-buried stash of ammunition, used by the Chinese military. The stash was too large to move quickly, but if the fire grew too close, the explosion would wipe out the settlement entirely.

Knowing the flames were following close on their heels, Yan's crew spent an hour clearing a fire break twice the length of a football field. By the time they were finished, the fire was towering over them like a crackling red wall. They leaped into their trucks and sped away, not wanting to be anywhere near the ammunition if it exploded. It didn't—their efforts were successful.

But the city of Xilinji couldn't be saved. By the time Yan reached it, black smoke choked the streets and the massive lumberyard was on fire. Sure he was about to die, Yan none-theless sent his truck careening into the chaos. His crew followed in five other vehicles. Struggling to breathe and to see, they scooped up as many people as possible, and headed back toward safety. By that time, the smoke was so thick that men had to get out of the trucks and walk in front of them to guide the drivers.

One truck was demolished by the flames, but Yan's crew managed to save themselves and 200 women and children.

Flash Facts

In June 1940, 1488 lightning fires were sparked over a 10-day period in Montana—a record-breaking streak of flashes and fire.

Bearing the scars of burns on their faces and hands, the firefighters were later hailed as heroes.

Thanks to the efforts of people like Yan, fewer than 200 people were killed in the disaster. But though they could save most of the inhabitants, they couldn't save the trees. The flames scoured the Chinese and Soviet sides of the river for more than a month, consuming an area larger than Scotland. In some places, temperatures rose high enough to warp and twist railway tracks. The land was left a charred wasteland, waiting for the slow repopulation of new plants and trees.

REBIRTH

While a forest like the Great Black Dragon doesn't regrow in a heartbeat—or even in a decade—fires do bring regeneration to the land. And many plants and animals have actually adapted themselves to the forest's cycle of fire and rebirth.

In western North America, lodgepole pines drop pine cones year after year, but many of the cones remain dormant. Their chambers are sealed by hardened pitch, called resin. In the heat of a forest fire, the resin melts, releasing new seeds onto the forest floor. The black soot created by the fire absorbs the heat of the sun and creates ideal growing conditions. Fertilized by ash, the seeds soon flourish.

Aspen also benefit from forest fires. Usually, once aspen trees are mature, the leaves send a hormone to the roots, stopping new growth and saving the available nutrients for the existing branches. But when the trees are singed or burned, the leaves no longer send the hormone, and new shoots soon appear. Perhaps aspen trees can sense that fires leave new minerals and new nutrients in the soil.

On the mountain slopes of British Columbia and the western United States, the ponderosa pine has adapted to life in dry summer forests, where lightning strikes cause wildfires every year. Tall and stately, the pines can live for centuries; one in Colorado lived for 1047 years. Obviously, a tree that old will have to weather at least a few flames. So, the species has adapted to survive all but the worst rage of a fire. Its bark is thick and the lower trunk has few branches, to keep flames from climbing to the canopy. And each tree has a deep root, to survive far below the heat of a fire. In some ways, occasional fires actually benefit the pines, by clearing the forest floor of needles and killing smaller trees that might compete for soil and sunlight.

In Australia, the grasstree can live for up to 600 years, slowly building a thick brown trunk of old leaf stems, glued together with resin. Yet only after a fire does the plant flower, releasing seeds for a new generation.

Other plants seem to use more subtle techniques to ensure that fires clear and fertilize the land. In California, the chamise, or greasewood, has strong roots that allow it to flourish quickly after a fire, choking out competing plant life. To give itself the best chance at its ideal, post-fire habitat, the bush drops leaves and branches as it grows until it's surrounded by a collection of kindling. The chemical make-up of the leaves actually changes as well—more and more resin and flammable material is stored as the plant ages. By the time it's mature, the plant is like a perfectly built campfire, complete with kindling, just waiting for a match—or lightning—to strike.

Animals have also adapted to forest fires. In the 1960s, a Canadian scientist named William George Evans started studying the body of a beetle that had happened to land near his dinner plate in a restaurant. The bug was a black fire beetle, known in other parts of the world as a jewel beetle. When he looked closely at the tiny indentations on the beetle's body,

Evans became convinced that the beetle had infrared sensors that could detect heat. Of course, no one believed him.

It wasn't until German scientists confirmed his theories more than four decades later that people actually accepted that fire beetles could see, hear, and sense heat from great distances—possibly several kilometers. Once they detected a blaze, the beetles would head directly toward the charred areas to mate and lay their eggs. There, in the still-smoldering coals of a burned log, the larvae could hatch without competition from other species.

Still other species rely on the ways that fires mold the forest landscape. The California condor, for example, is the largest

Hot Ideas

After Dr. Helmut Schmitz at the University of Bonn in Germany confirmed that fire beetles used infrared information, scientists began developing new kinds of infrared sensors, inspired by the bug's highly sensitive detectors. The United States military is watching the research closely. If they're successful, the tiny sensors could replace the larger ones now used on heat-seeking missiles.

bird in North America. It weighs about as much as a two-year-old child and has a wingspan longer than a pickup truck. Yet this massive bird is teetering at the edge of extinction and biologists believe that fire suppression is partly to blame.

In the forests of Arizona, Mexico, and southern California, where the bird traditionally nests, foresters have been so good at controlling wildfires that the woods have grown dense and filled with underbrush. The open meadows where condors could once hunt field mice and squirrels are no longer as common. Now, they pick at the bodies of dead animals the same way that vultures do. But the lack of tiny field mice bones to crunch has led to a lack of calcium in the condors' diet, and their eggshells are too thin to protect the tiny lives within. If the young birds manage to hatch, their bones are often weak. To survive alongside humans and their fire-fighting habits, condors are going to have to find a new source of calcium. Today, teams of biologists are working to help save the birds from extinction.

Coaxing Condors Back to Life

By capturing some of the last breeding birds and strictly controlling their diets, scientists are trying to save the condor species. There are now about 90 in the wild, and about 125 living in captivity.

More and more scientists are finding that forest fires actually help some species. In 1998, researchers began tracking bird populations in two Alberta forests—one old-growth area and one area recently burned by a forest fire. They immediately counted more birds in the burned forest. Then, over the next three years, they found the bird population there steadily increasing, while the population in the old-growth forest remained the same.

The answer, they suggested, lay inside the dead, half-burned timber. There, wood-eating beetles were busy munching away. The beetles, in turn, provided a steady diet for the birds. Two of the most successful species were black-beaked and three-toed woodpeckers. These birds blended in to the dark colors of the charred trees, and used their tough beaks to flake through the damaged bark for the bugs inside. And because woodpeckers don't migrate, they could feast on forest-fire remains all year round.

After the massive fires in Yellowstone National Park, American scientists launched more than 200 research projects. Among other things, they found that the elk population quickly rebounded, feeding on new growth. Snowshoe hares thrived in the new open grasslands and the lynx population increased as the wildcats hunted the hares. Large birds such as owls and hawks also benefited—it was easier for them to see their prey on the open forest floor.

Although the fires had been unbelievably destructive, they had also left behind open space, fertilized soil, and fresh young growth to feed the surviving animals. Just as the wrath of the Hawaiian volcanoes helped create new land, the fires of Yellowstone National Park reinvented the forest.

Reborn in the Ashes

Winter after winter after winter.

For three years, the ice won't melt. Driven mad by the cold and the darkness, families and tribes will tear themselves apart and leaders will feud. The wolves that chase the sun and the moon through the sky each day will finally catch their quarry, and the world will be plunged into permanent darkness. Even the stars will disappear. Led by their ruler Surtr, giants will escape from the realm of fire and advance over the earth, leaving everything in their paths in flames. On a massive battlefield, they will be joined by other monsters, and they will wait for battle.

The gods will respond to the challenge. Odin and Thor and other heroes of legend will fly to the defense of the world, using all their might against the giants. But though they face their fates with infinite courage, they are predestined to fail.

As the giants win the battle, Surtr will burn the entire world. He will set the land and the sky on fire, until the earth sinks into the ocean. But not even Surtr will have the power to extinguish life completely. After many years the sun will reappear and give birth to a beautiful daughter, who will take her place in the sky. A few gods will survive. And two humans who hid in a magical forest to escape the fires will emerge and have children.

The end of the world as told in Nordic mythology is violent and dark. But it carries the hope of renewal, as well. Even the most powerful, destructive beings can only temporarily devastate the land—they can't extinguish life.

There are many such stories of death and rebirth through flames. In ancient Egyptian mythology, the red and gold phoenix lived for 500 years. Then it built itself a nest of cinnamon sticks, carefully arranged to catch the sun's rays. Once the sun had set the nest on fire, the phoenix beat its wings to fan the flames until it was consumed in the blaze. Out of the ashes, a newborn phoenix rose.

The legends of Europe are populated by smoke-belching, fire-breathing dragons. In Poland, the dragon Smok ravaged the countryside and devoured young girls until a shoemaker's apprentice tricked the creature into drinking so much water that it exploded. In British mythology, countless knights risked their lives and dared the fires to prove their bravery and chivalry. Yet these same dragons were often the guardians of fantastical treasure. In Finland, someone who found the mating place of dragons could steal a brilliant white stone and dash toward the nearest water. If he reached the water before the dragons killed him, he was granted extra intelligence and cunning for the rest of his life.

To the Icelandic storytellers who wove tales during long Arctic nights, the Egyptians who worshipped the immortality of a bird who died and was born out of flames, or the Europeans who scanned the skies for scaled, treasure-hording dragons, fires had a dual meaning. They were both deadly and immortal. They were destructive and awe-inspiring. They were symbols of complete chaos and signs of new beginnings.

We find the same themes in other fire stories, of both actual occurrences and human tales. The forests of Yellowstone National Park changed and thrived after forest fires seared through; the ritual sacrificial fires of the Aztecs brought forth the sun for a new half-century. Even the deadly power of nitroglycerin has now been turned to medical uses. When a tiny amount is given to people suffering heart attacks, it enlarges the veins and allows the heart muscle to pump less vigorously.

In modern times, we may no longer worship fire—we may even forget its presence in our daily lives—but we still haven't learned to control its power. We can be caught unaware, confused by smoke, and ambushed by heat. Fire remains as explosive as gunpowder and as hot as the blacksmith's forge, as unpredictable as a lightning strike and as wild as Pele's volcanic temper.

And yet, flames can still be a reason to celebrate. At Halloween, people light jack-o-lanterns and walk through decorated streets waving flashlights and glow sticks. In Asia, they guide spirits with glowing festival lanterns. Athletes even carry an Olympic torch around the world. And when fireworks burst in the sky, people leave their private homes and gather to watch.

The roots of many pyrotechnic traditions lie in the idea that loud noises and bright lights can scare bad spirits away. That makes fireworks an ideal way to "clear the air" and welcome a new year. In China, people have been celebrating the lunar new year this way ever since fireworks were invented. In India, Deepavali is a time of rejoicing, in memory of the god Rama conquering the demon Ravana. Fireworks in every imaginable size and shape are set off in parks and squares and even neighborhood streets, part of the year's most exuberant festival.

In other regions of the world, the spiritual connotations have faded away, but the New Year's Eve fireworks have continued. People see the explosions above Seattle's Space Needle, Sydney's harbor, or Ottawa's Parliament Buildings as part of one enormous celebration. In New York's Times Square, over a million people gather to watch the explosions, while millions more watch on television. For audiences around the world, the explosions mark a time to gather with friends, family—or even with crowds of strangers—and talk about hopes for the year to come.

Fireworks celebrations have spread to other parts of the year as well. Every summer in Montréal, the L'International des Feux Loto-Québec, or the Montréal Fireworks Festival, brings top pyrotechnic companies to the world's largest competition. Employing some of the same technologies that

Ancient Wisdom

In the first century, Greek philosopher and historian Pliny the Elder recognized fire's dual nature, writing that "fire is the immeasurable, uncontrollable element . . . It is hard to say whether it consumes more or produces more." He died at age 56, suffocated by poisonous gases while he was studying a volcano.

Chinese engineers used to impress 11th-century emperors, these teams send blast after blast of fireworks into the sky, timing each explosion to match the beat of popular or classical music. For Montréal residents, the event is an excuse to leave their homes and cluster on the banks of the St. Lawrence River to watch the displays. On most nights, more than 2 million people gather. Children stay up long past their bedtimes, lovers curl up on picnic blankets, and riverside businesses open their balconies to overflowing crowds.

Thousands of years ago, a central fire had the power to attract people, to gather them around a central source of light and warmth. Today, when most of us live more solitary lives and spend the evenings in small family groups, a fireworks display can draw us outside to gather with our neighbors. It creates a sense of community, the same way a bonfire does. And just as the first hearth fire did in prehistoric times, the splendor of fireworks on a dark night sparks awe and wonder within us all.

SOURCES

Anderson, Johannes C. *Myths and Legends of the Polynesians.* Rutland, VT: Charles E. Tuttle, 1969.

Appenzeller, Tim. "The Coal Paradox." *National Geographic.* March 2006: 98.

Beddoes, J. and M.J. Bibby. *Principles of Metal Manufacturing Processes.* London: Arnold, 1999.

Brown, Stephen R. *A Most Damnable Invention.* Toronto: Viking Canada, 2005.

"The Cities: The Price of Optimism." *Time.* August 1, 1969: 39–41.

Cromie, William J. "Cooking Up Quite a Story." *Harvard University Gazette.* June 13, 2002.

Faith, Nicholas. *Blaze.* New York: St. Martin's Press, 1999.

Flint, William. "A History of U.S. Lightships." From U.S. Coast Guard website. www.uscg.mil/history/h_lightships.html.

Hawley, John Stratton. *Sati, the Blessing and the Curse.* Oxford: Oxford University Press, 1994.

Hibben, Thomas. *The Sons of Vulcan.* Philadelphia: J.B. Lippencott, 1940.

Jones, David E. *An Instinct for Dragons.* New York: Routledge, 2000.

Kelly, Jack. *Gunpowder.* New York: Basic Books, 2004.

Lawson, John A. *A New Voyage to Carolina.* Champaign, IL: Project Gutenberg, 1711.

Levack, Brian P. *The Witch-Hunt in Early Modern Europe.* Harlow: Pearson Education, 1995.

"Lightning: The Shocking Story." From the website of National Geographic Kids. www.nationalgeographic.com/lightning.

Lucas, A. and J.R. Harris. *Ancient Egyptian Materials and Industries.* New York: Dover Publications, 1999.

Marley, Karin. "We Can't Stop Playing with our Food." *Maclean's.* August 18, 2005: 36–37.

McBride, Michele. *The Fire That Will Not Die*. Palm Springs: ETC Publications, 1979.

Newton, David E. *Encyclopedia of Fire*. Westport, CT: Oryx Press, 2002.

Partington, J.R. *A History of Greek Fire and Gunpowder*. Baltimore: The Johns Hopkins University Press, 1999.

Pyne, Stephen J. *Vestal Fire*. Seattle: University of Washington Press, 1997.

Pyne, Stephen J. *World Fire*. New York: Henry Holt & Co., 1995.

Rehder, J.E. *The Mastery and Uses of Fire in Antiquity*. Montreal: McGill-Queen's University Press, 2000.

Rosi, Mauro; Paulo Papale; Luca Lupi; and Marco Stoppato. *Volcanoes*. Toronto: Firefly Books, 2003.

Rossoti, Hazel. *Fire*. Oxford: Oxford University Press, 1993.

Salisbury, Harrison E. *The Great Black Dragon Fire*. Boston: Little, Brown & Co., 1989.

"Solar Physics." From Marshall Space Flight Center website. http://solarscience.msfc.nasa.gov/SunspotCycle.shtml

Turner, Alice K. *The History of Hell*. New York: Harcourt Brace & Co., 1993.

White, Ellen Emerson. "Profiling Arsonists and Their Motives." *Fire Engineering*. March 1996: 80.

Willer, Brian. "A Life of Risks to Save Lives." *Maclean's*. December 30, 1991.

Williams, Peter. *Beacon on the Rock*. Edinburgh: Birlinn, 2001.

Winchester, Simon. *Krakatoa*. New York: HarperCollins, 2003.

INDEX

ABOUT THE AUTHOR

Tanya Lloyd Kyi has been interested in fire ever since she and her friend Michelle worked together on a grade 8 science fair project about lightning. They used a static generator, cotton balls, and a small figurine of a golfer to show how lightning worked. Unfortunately, the cotton-ball clouds turned out to be flammable. The innocent golfer was not only struck by lightning, but also somewhat melted by the flames.

Tanya has managed to survive most of her life without setting any more fires, except for one small incident with the Christmas turkey in 2001. She is the author of *Fires!*, *Rescues!*, *Jared Lester: Fifth Grade Jester*, and *The Blue Jean Book*, which won the Christie Harris Illustrated Children's Literature Prize. She lives in Vancouver, BC.

OTHER BOOKS BY TANYA LLOYD KYI

Jared Lester, Fifth-Grade Jester
Jared wants to be a jester, but where will he perform, with no royal court around? This is a charming and humorous tale of a boy's determination to realize his dream.

True Stories from the Edge: Rescues!
Whether they are trained rescue workers or simply passersby, the brave people in these ten stories defy the odds in times of grave danger.

True Stories from the Edge: Fires!
Step into the blinding flames, the choking smoke, and the waves of heat that have brought humans face-to-face with one of the world's mightiest natural forces.

The Blue Jean Book
◆ Society of School Librarians International Honor Book Award
◆ NYPL Books for the Teen Age selection
◆ International Youth Library White Ravens selection
◆ Our Choice starred selection
◆ Christie Harris Illustrated Children's Literature Prize
◆ Children's Literature Roundtables of Canada's 2006 Information Book Award, finalist
◆ Red Maple Award nominee

Discover the fascinating story of denim's rise from its origins with hardscrabble miners and cowboys, to its popularity among laborers, rebels, and the incurably hip.